# TERRORIST
# SPECTACULARS

A Twentieth Century Fund Paper

# Should TV Coverage Be Curbed?

## by MICHAEL J. O'NEILL

PP Priority Press Publications/New York/1986

The Twentieth Century Fund is an independent research foundation which undertakes policy studies of economic, political, and social institutions and issues. The Fund was founded in 1919 and endowed by Edward A. Filene.

# Foreword

Technology has a great deal to do with the rise of modern terrorism. Terrorists these days have a large armory at their disposal, from the most rudimentary Molotov cocktails to some of the most advanced electronic remote control devices. They have acquired skills in using other new technologies. Among their accomplishments is an increasingly astute exploitation of the electronic media, specifically television, in pursuit of their aims.

Terrorism is not new, but in the past it existed mainly in the shadows. Those who resorted to violence usually concentrated on political or military figures. In some places terrorists continue to use this traditional tactic. But others now aim their fire at innocent civilians. The bombings, usually by dynamite-laden autos, in Beirut; the explosion in Harrod's, London's great department store, in the midst of the Christmas season; and the random shootings in airports and airplanes have claimed many innocent victims. Whenever these incidents take place, ubiquitous television camera teams are quickly on the scene, providing gory and dramatic views of the tragic carnage.

Television has played an even bigger role in airplane hijackings. In such cases, terrorists have often come out of the dark to appear on the screen, either to make demands or plead their cause. These attempts, it should be pointed out, are almost exclusively designed to move the hearts and minds of people in the Western democracies. Authoritarian regimes would not allow their television screens to be used for such antics, nor are the terrorists interested in swaying such regimes. To the contrary, they have learned that Western television, with its competitive spirit, its zest for violence, and its technical efficiency in covering it, can sometimes serve as the unwitting handmaiden or tool of terrorism.

Both the staff and Trustees of the Twentieth Century Fund have long been troubled by this new phenomenon that seemingly links television with terrorism. As defenders of press freedom, we have been opposed to restrictions on the press, including television news departments. Television, though, often goes to excess, dwelling on the plight of the hostages and their families and allowing terrorists to look more like freedom fighters than common criminals. We have always believed—and continue to believe—that the viewing public can distinguish between television as a medium for delivering a message and the message itself. But we also recognize that the television camera can distort, even lie, presenting what might be called the acceptable face of terrorism on a screen blocking out, at least momentarily, the ugly and unacceptable reality.

We asked Michael J. O'Neill, a veteran print journalist and former editor of New York's *Daily News* and former president of the American Society of Newspaper Editors (ASNE), to ponder some of the dilemmas posed by television coverage of terrorism. In his thoughtful and provocative paper, he has done an admirable job of examining the difficulties that a free press faces in dealing with terrorist outrages, particularly those involving innocent hostages. I think that his views, and his suggestions for reform, are illuminating and instructive. His contribution may strike some television practitioners as controversial. But this is a constructive contribution, and one that should be widely debated. I congratulate him for it.

M. J. Rossant, DIRECTOR
The Twentieth Century Fund
August 1986

# Contents

**Foreword** by M. J. Rossant          *v*

Preface          1
1 / News from the Stars          3
2 / Why Television Is So Different      15
3 / Television in Captivity      23
4 / Television, Terror, and Policy      39
5 / A Better Way      57
6 / Government and Public Opinion      79
7 / Preventive Journalism      101
Notes      105

# Preface

Criticism is often a form of rebellion. It is aimed at the overthrow of prevailing ideas rather than presiding governments, although that sometimes follows. It is a popular pursuit because it is much safer than revolution—very few critics are shot, in free societies at least—and it is just as satisfying to the ego. Indeed, it is hard to imagine anything more satisfying because the critic is constantly celebrating the superiority of his own views over everyone else's while taking no responsibility for what is right or wrong in the world and seldom being called to account for his own errors. Many professional intellectuals, for example, now champion neo-conservative thinking and cold war policies with the same claim of infallibility they made when they lobbied for Marxism in the 1930s and 1940s.

Another appealing fact about criticism is the custom of focusing on other people and institutions rather than looking in a mirror. I remember Governor Hugh Carey complaining once that the New York City newspapers were in no position to attack his handling of a labor dispute when they had just made a complete hash of their own union negotiations. "Governor," I explained, "our speciality is giving advice to others, not following it ourselves." The media are the critics of everything around them, they are the marketplace where all that government does is constantly challenged and debated, yet they recoil from criticism of their own performance.

Although I share this journalistic weakness, I have tried in the present essay to subject the coverage of terrorism to the same kind of critical analysis that reporters apply to others. I am conscious, however, of at least one vulnerability: the emphasis on television's curious relationship to terrorism and the comparatively little attention paid to newspapers. This might be seen as a

1

print journalist's prejudice against a rival but it is not. It is neither an exoneration of newspaper failings nor a put-down of television where a Walter Cronkite or a John Chancellor can match talents with anyone in print. It is simply recognition of a fundamental fact: In terrorist incidents, television is now overwhelmingly the dominant medium. It mobilizes public emotions, influences government policies, and even shapes the events themselves. Of necessity, it is the centerpiece in any discussion of coverage problems.

Murray J. Rossant's original assignment was to explore the conflict in terrorist cases between the full exercise of press freedoms on the one hand and society's need to protect itself on the other. The intent was not to condemn but to illumine and, through illumination, to discover how news practices could be reformed to better serve the public without injuring its right to be fully informed. To reform, of course, is to rebel against what exists, in this case to overthrow some old reportorial habits, and that is the rub. As John Maynard Keynes observed, "The difficulty lies, not in the new ideas, but in escaping from the old ones." This is the great challenge in the coverage of terrorism; it is a challenge journalism must overcome in its own long-term best interest.

I am indebted to a number of people for their generous assistance. Neil C. Livingstone and Terrell E. Arnold, nationally recognized authorities on terrorism, were invaluable guides in every aspect of the general problem. John Chancellor, Robert C. Christopher, Fred Friendly, and Richard Clurman provided a great deal of sound journalistic advice, but remain innocent of any surviving flaws (some of Chancellor's reservations never were resolved). Jack Metcalfe edited and corrected the copy with painstaking care. Jane Maxwell of ABC, James F. Plante of NBC, and Ann Morfoten of CBS generously mobilized scripts and other network materials. Murray Rossant, Marcia Bystryn, Beverly Goldberg, Scott McConnell, and their staffs at the Twentieth Century Fund, were enormously helpful and supportive. And, as always, my wife and fellow journalist was a rich source of editorial candor and general wisdom.

# 1 / News from the Stars

Remember that incredible day in June 1985 . . . about 10:30 in the morning . . . the Boeing 727 sitting on the tarmac at the airport in Beirut . . . and the pilot, John Testrake, leaning out of his cockpit window while a terrorist held a pistol to his head and clamped a hand over his mouth.

A scene spread across millions of television screens—not flesh and blood, nothing anyone could touch, just flickering photons rushing through quiet living rooms and bars and the Oval Office, inanimate, impersonal but sending strong emotions coiling around the temper of the nation. Anger, frustration, the urge to strike back, to get revenge.

REPORTER: Thank you, Captain. How do you feel?

TESTRAKE: All right.

The same picture seen in the United States also appearing in Lebanon, Israel, all through the Middle East and North Africa, and spreading across Europe—mobilizing human feelings on a massive scale, elation as well as anger, satisfaction as well as frustration, feelings of triumph in one place and dismay in another. Everywhere, private and public opinion set in motion, official policies and priorities rearranged. All of this at the same time, in a matter of minutes or hours.

REPORTER: Captain, many people in America are calling for some kind of a rescue operation or some kind of retaliation. Do you have any thoughts on that?

TESTRAKE: I think that we'd all be dead men if they did because we're continually surrounded by many, many guards.

REPORTER: Do you have any thoughts on whether or not the United States should ask Israel to release the people it's holding in Israel?

TESTRAKE: No, I won't comment.

3

At one point, a terrorist jerked the pilot back into the cockpit. Minutes later a jittery captor fired through a plane window and another gunman outside, shouting "Trick! Journalist!" unloaded his AK-47 assault rifle over the heads of reporters jostling toward the tarmac from the terminal building. So violence and quiet conversation mingled together in a single experience shared by tens of millions of people. It was a moment crowded with incredible contrasts, a bizarre juxtaposition of opposites, and irony. Most of all, irony.

There they were, two ABC reporters, Charles Glass and Julie Flint, standing under the nose of the plane asking questions while their camera rolled, just as if they were doing a stand-up on the White House lawn, free people in the outside world, able to leave whenever they wished. And only a few feet away, the three crewmen in the plane, not free to leave, not even free to say what they wanted to, held in a tiny, hostile world guarded by Shiite gunmen.

The gunmen themselves were engaged in an ancient form of unconventional warfare, as old as the human race, well known to Sennacherib and Caesar, to the original Assassins in eleventh century Persia and Syria, and more recently to the victims of an Abu Nidal or Moammar Gaddafi. But finally in Beirut the ancient and the new were strangely joined, primordial fear linked to jetliners and television cameras, the products of human progress placed in the service of primitive terrorism.

In another irony, faithful Muslims committed murder during the holy month of Ramadan. They brutally beat the navy diver, Robert Dean Stethem, shot him in the head, and then dumped his battered body on a runway, claiming to be acting in the name of "God, the Merciful, the Compassionate." Apparently they never saw any contradiction.

The terrorists were members of the Hizbollah or "Party of God," militant Lebanese Shiites acting "under the patronage" of Iran's Ayatollah Khomeini and waging a jihad to defeat "the imams of infidelity in America, France and Israel." In an "Open Letter" or manifesto, the Hizbollah said its mission was to stamp out Western ideas, which "cannot respond to man's aspirations," and to return all Muslims to their ancient faith because "only Islam can bring about man's renaissance, progress and creativity."[1] But in Beirut, these same missionaries of the seventh century turned away from the past and joined forces with the most modern form of Western cultural aggression—television.

## Hucksters of Terror

Nabih Berri, leader of the powerful Amal, the main Shiite group in Lebanon, moved into the crisis with the smooth assurance of a European diplomat, well-dressed, clean-shaven, and "looking more like a rug merchant than a terrorist," in the words of Christopher Dickey of the *Washington Post*. He was a lawyer. He held a green card which he used regularly for easy entry into the country to visit his former American wife and six children in Dearborn, Michigan. He knew American ways and the American media as well as he knew the politics of violence.

Many of the other Amal leaders also had close ties to the United States. They once lived and studied here, still had families in the country and telephoned them frequently. They grew up with television in West Beirut and had been in regular contact with the media during Lebanon's civil war. Even the newest Amal recruit knew he was supposed to act ferocious whenever he saw a television camera. Nicholas Livingston of the Associated Press remembers his trips to check the Green Line in Beirut: "I'd often see the fighters lounging about, smoking hash or just talking. Then a TV crew would show up. Suddenly, they would all start shooting across the line. Other fighters would shoot back and, intrepid reporter that I am, I'd head back to the office." Even without a director, the action was supplied on cue, reality served up instantly for the camera, like a Big Mac at MacDonald's.

Even the myth-shrouded Iranian Musa al Sadr, revered Imam of the Lebanese Shia who disappeared in Libya like the legendary Twelfth Imam in 873, was not so burdened with spiritual duties or so immersed in the past that he did not concern himself with the media. In a private comment to a colleague regarding the PLO enemy, he once observed: "With weapons Arafat gets money; with money he can feed the press; and thanks to the press he can get a hearing before world public opinion."[2] Clearly, the downtrodden Shiites intended to use modern media as well as state-of-the-art weapons to seek their day in the political sun.

So it was no surprise in the TWA crisis that the Shia Amal quickly took over the American networks, helping to script, direct, and produce the entire drama. For two tumultuous weeks, Berri and his media-savvy lieutenants staged photo opportunities, laid on press conferences, supplied hostages for interviews, and hawked tips, inside information, and even film tapes like *bazaaris*. Berri himself used American television to broadcast his litany of Shiite grievances, sent messages to Ronald Reagan and to Shimon Peres, negotiated with Dan Rather of CBS and David Hartman of ABC, chatted with anchormen and other media celebrities, and even offered fatherly assurances to the worried wife of hostage Allyn Conwell.

In a crazy scene only modern electronics could deliver, Hartman in New York was on an audio circuit with Olga Conwell in Cyprus, who was talking live to her husband while he was being held under guard in Berri's barricaded Beirut home. At one point, Conwell suddenly said, "Hold on honey, let me let you speak to Mr. Berri." Then, while the world listened in, the Amal leader himself came on the line, called her "Olga" as if she were an old friend, and said, "I will take care of your husband." In a final touch, a telephone operator broke in to ask, "Are you through? Mr. Berri . . . ?" Just another one of those moments when you "reach out and touch someone."

The networks, of course, played their assigned roles to the hilt, with the competitive frenzy they reserve for all big stories, when even the anchormen we have chosen to lead the nation, those calm, assured symbols of all wisdom, suddenly begin acting "like dogs in heat," as Peter Jennings of ABC so delicately put it. In these conditions, the rating stakes are high, competition is fierce, the pressures for scoops intense, and the scramble for advantage sometimes riotous. So riotous that during one press conference the armed terrorists had to retreat in disorder with their hostages before a mob of jostling, screaming newsmen. "It was a disgrace," said Rather, an unflattering image of journalism in action that wasn't supposed to be put on the air. Reporters, who expose others but like to shield themselves, immediately rushed to their own defense, laying all the blame on foreign photographers, mostly French, who naturally were never interviewed for their side of the incident.

The whole TWA drama was, of course, a sorry spectacle, a classic study in irony and contrast, in the deadly attraction that extremes have for one another, like prisoners for their captors. The television networks, the offspring of Western technology and ideas, champions of democratic freedoms and rights, were working with Muslim terrorists in the theater of the absurd, dealing with gunmen who had kidnapped and murdered Americans. They were being manipulated, they admitted, used to promote the Amal cause and to pressure Israel into releasing 766 Shiite prisoners. Although they claimed television coverage helped save hostage lives, they conceded it might also promote new acts of

terror. But they said they had to do what they did—more irony—
in the interest of an informed public, in the name of a free press.

The media critics swarmed to the attack during the TWA hijacking, led by Henry Kissinger, a television star in his own right,
who conducted shuttle punditry like shuttle diplomacy, hurry-
ing from network to network and from talk show to evening news
program, contributing to the general melee by denouncing his
hosts' behavior in Beirut. He said it was "indecent" to show
Americans "on display, under the control of terrorists," or to sur-
render television to "the kidnappers of Americans" so that they
could "spread their propaganda."[3] John Corry of *The New York
Times* and David Broder of the *Washington Post*, who never made
it to the networks because they are not certified celebrities,
leveled similar charges in a less visible way. "Terrorism is a form
of warfare," said Broder; it shouldn't have "access to mass media
outlets."[4] So the networks were left in the dock, accused of giving the terrorists too much exposure, of humanizing and hyping the crisis so that the government was forced to respond to
immediate public pressures rather than act in the longer-term
best interests of the nation.

### Circle Theory of Behavior

Television's alliance with terror may seem bizarre. In fact,
however, the strange joining of opposites is a natural
phenomenon; it is totally consistent with the circle theory of
human behavior. This theory is a paradox which states that the
further people move away from each other in philosophy,
politics, ideology, religion, temperament, or almost anything
else, the closer they come together. As their views become more
and more extreme—left or right, liberal or conservative, progressive or reactionary—the distance between them seems to ex-
pand. But they actually are being drawn around in a great circle,
much like Einstein's bending light, until they finally arrive at
exactly the same spot.

The result is that one can hardly distinguish between a Fascist
and Communist dictator. Radical leftists are usually just as in-
tolerant of dissent as right-wing extremists, just as ruthless in
stamping out opposition. So as the circle closes, a Castro merges
with a Batista, an Ortega with a Somoza. Although the levels
of violence are different, the fanaticism of an Abu Nidal and
a Meir Kehane is a shared amalgam of hate. The Soviets attack
religion and the Ayatollah imposes religion with the same

repressive methods. And Muslim leaders use modern ideas and modern technology to speed their flight from the Western modernism they condemn.

In a different way, the same theory applies in the wondrous world of television where the lines of magnetic force also move through our lives in a circular field. For in television, reality and fiction, which are supposed to stand apart, far enough apart at least to be distinguished one from the other, are often driven around the circle until they merge in the nation's confused perception. When reality has to be rearranged, embellished, and dramatized to meet the demands of theater, when it is pumped up with emotional hype and styled for celebrity anchors, it loses much of its essence. It drifts toward fiction. And at the other end of the scale, when events are staged—firefights produced on cue and hostages speaking lines they do not mean—it is a case of fiction putting on the mask of reality, a kind of docudrama like the one about Edward R. Murrow that so outraged CBS news veterans.

During its morning news on June 17, CBS opened with a tease showing the released hostage Robert Peel while he described the TWA ordeal: "American people on that plane have just about had it. That plane is a pigpen. They're exhausted. They've had water and bread for three days. . . . All their money's gone. Their jewelry's been taken, their travelers' checks. . . . It's just pure hell on there right now."

This injection of adrenalin was followed during the next two hours by a whole series of news bulletins and interviews, all on the TWA crisis. Every time the emotional stimulation seemed to wear off, usually just before commercial announcements when viewers are especially vulnerable to distraction, the producers gave everyone a booster; they cut to a tape of a freed hostage.

WOMAN: I didn't want to get off. . . . I didn't want to go without him. He wanted me to go. So—(weeping)—when we get home, we're getting married.

### News Theater

These poignant scenes were repeated again and again. The purpose was not to report new developments in the story, because the hostages had been interviewed the night before. It was not to fulfill journalism's duty to keep the American public informed; the public already had the news. It was simply and purely a theatrical device, little pieces of human stress cut out of reality, rearranged and pasted together again for maximum entertainment effect—all to stimulate the emotions of viewers and keep them riveted to the CBS channel.

Eventually, the hostages were freed and returned to the United States in an orgy of televised celebration, interviews, and family reunions, some of which were financed by television producers eager for exclusives. Said Steve Friedman, producer of the "Today Show," "We are asking these people to do things for us and we are helping them out in return"—just as simple as that.[5] The armada of television crews and newspaper reporters checked out of the Commodore, Summerland, and other hotels in Beirut. Once again the city was left alone with its own fraternal violence, forgotten by the American media as quickly as it was remembered when the hijacking began—until some new outrage would start the cycle all over again.

Three months later, after Israeli planes had bombed the PLO headquarters in Tunisia, four Palestinian terrorists hijacked the Italian liner *Achille Lauro* in an operation believed to have been masterminded by the notorious Muhammad Abbas. An American tourist was shot to death in his wheelchair, and more than 400 passengers and crew were taken hostage. In November, a plane with 98 aboard was hijacked en route from Athens to Cairo and 60 people ultimately died at the hands of the Palestinian terrorists or during a shoot-out with Egyptian commandos on Malta. And then, just two days after Christmas, terrorists attacked the Rome and Vienna airports, leaving 19 dead and 114 wounded.

In all three episodes, the television coverage was more restrained than in the TWA case, and news executives began talking about the lessons they had applied from their experience in Beirut. But the circumstances were far different; the new attacks simply did not provide the networks with enough dramatic material for a TWA rerun. In the *Achille Lauro* case, the terrorists and the hostages were on board a ship, cut off from television cameras, with only scratchy radio transmissions intermittently linking reporters to the events at sea. There were no gun-covered press conferences and no personalities like Berri to focus on. Only newscasters and the usual talking heads, the officials and experts who at the wiggle of a producer's ears instantly assemble around disaster, like paid mourners at a funeral.

Rather applied heavy makeup to his language to create the illusion of drama, opening his show one night with: "The voice of terror at sea. 'Meet our demands or we will kill.' In Cairo, the voice of relief. The ship passengers who got away. In America, the voice of fear and frustration for those still held at the point of a gun."

But colorful words could not make up for the missing pictures. Also, there was no suspense to mobilize emotions. The crisis ended after only two days, the surviving hostages set free and the hijackers allowed to disappear. It was a big story, but as television drama it did not match Beirut. No one could tell, therefore, what lessons television had learned or applied.

Columbia University's Fred Friendly, Murrow's onetime producer at CBS, was not optimistic. After years in the business, he said, he had concluded he should be "a citizen first and a journalist second" and put national interest ahead of competitive enterprise in the coverage of terrorism. But he did not expect his colleagues to follow. He noted that after the Iranian hostage experience, the networks had said "we'll do it better next time" but then in the TWA case forgot all their promises.[6] They made new resolutions after the TWA crisis, but it was probable that these, too, would falter when put to a new test and that competitive frenzy would again overwhelm the consciences of the kings and make cowards of them all.

### Issues Unresolved

The central fact is that the public issues which the TWA case exposed in such grotesque detail still stand before us. After the hijacking, there was an immediate rush of speeches, seminars, congressional hearings, and professional arguments, all the way from Los Angeles to London and Jerusalem, from newspaper city rooms to those West Side bars where broadcasters hang out in New York. Television executives admitted excesses in Beirut but otherwise rose nobly to their own defense, arguing that television was not collaborating with terrorists, just covering terrorism the way it covers any other news, that its behavior is determined by the nature of news, the nature of television, and the fact that in a democratic society journalists must be free, even to commit mayhem, so that they can serve the people's right to know. In other words, as Walter Cronkite used to say, "that's the way it is." Or is it?

Not exactly. The dilemmas for society and government, for journalism itself, are not so easily dispersed, because everything is not as it seems. For one thing, many of television's arguments are quicker than the mind. They are pulled out of the hat so fast we don't see the premises. Logic sweeps us along to conclusions that seem incontestable because we do not realize that some of the assumptions are illusions, like much that is on television. And one of these illusions is that television news is just the same as any other news defended by the Constitution, when in fact there are important differences.

### Television News Is Different

The definition of news, which has been based on print journalism, has changed over the years as newspapers have progressed from the raucously partisan journals of Revolutionary times—Jefferson said, "nothing can now be believed which can be seen in a newspaper"—to the beguiling "cult of objectivity," which became a vogue after World War II. News is only tenuously associated with the truth that the press always says it is pursuing because, as Walter Lippmann observed, reporters almost never know the truth. But it is supposed to be linked to reality and to the factual information that a democracy needs for its own governance. This is why the press was singled out for special protection under the First Amendment.

During its formative years, when techniques were primitive and equipment cumbersome, television followed the newspaper model in its approach to the news. But with advances in technology it soon began developing its great dramatic potential. It provided live coverage in living color. It produced newsmakers and celebrity correspondents on cue. It added entertainment, emotional impact, and theatrical manipulation to create a whole new kind of communication. This was not the news as print journalism had defined it. But it was still called news and it profoundly changed the whole culture of news coverage and newsmaking. In the process, it sent newspapers into decline, not so much in profits but in numbers and—worse—in prestige and political power.

As network anchormen became bigger than rock stars, summoning the great ones to their booths at any hour of the day or night, newspaper columnists had to settle for answering machines or, like William F. Buckley, Jr., they joined the enemy and created their own television shows. Washington hostesses would instantly drop columnist George Will out of their computer files if he ever lost his television stage. And mere reporters are knocked down all the time by politicians running to studios.

During the 1984 presidential campaign, Gary Hart was presiding over a strategy session at the Waldorf-Astoria Hotel in New York when he suddenly jumped up and hurried away. On his return, his surprised advisers asked why he had left. No emergency, the candidate replied, just that he had heard television cameras were gathering outside the room where French President Mitterrand was staying. It was a photo opportunity, and he had rushed to seize it. He would never have abandoned his meeting for a newspaper reporter.

Like American politicians, terrorists pay almost no attention to the print media, as Berri and associates demonstrated. Anchor Tom Brokaw interrupted an African safari and flew into Beirut to be the NBC "big foot," a "big foot" being a television star who tramples on his local correspondent to take over a major story. He said later he was almost embarrassed by the favored treatment television got, recalling particularly his encounters with a frustrated Christopher Dickey of the *Washington Post*, the newspaper that once helped to destroy a president. "I would come out of closed door meetings with the leaders," he said, "and he would be standing out in the hallway looking for tidbits. . . . Television had a great deal of access and my friends in print were standing not just outside but outside in the street."[7]

The point is not to take up a collection for the *Washington Post* or other newspapers. It is simply to suggest that television is the core problem in terror coverage and that there are fundamental differences between its news and print news. These differences critically affect the way the public judges performance in incidents like Flight 847. Despite the allure of network reasoning, the excesses and distorting effects of television cannot be dismissed as only the by-product of a free press in action. Deeper issues related to television's unique nature and powers are involved.

### Entertainment Corrupts

Television's claim to all the rights and privileges of the press club set up by the Constitution is undermined when it substitutes entertainment for news. Television news executives themselves freely concede the intrusion of theater into their work. They call their programs "shows" and their most popular performers "stars." They often cast blondes in anchor roles mainly because they are beautiful, not because they have the kind of reportorial experience that a Walter Cronkite or John Chancellor brought to their assignments. Talk show hosts roll around the news decks like loose cannon because their bosses are program directors rather than news producers. This was true of "Good Morning America" until Hartman slipped one day and asked Berri if he had "any final words" for President Reagan. It sounded like television conducting its own hostage negotiations so "Good Morning's" news was shifted abruptly from the entertainment division to ABC news.

The incident highlighted another weakness in television's assertion of First Amendment rights. Because of its show biz character, its emphasis on stars and glamour, its attraction for media-hungry public figures, it is forever getting into the middle of events. Instead of merely covering the news, it often becomes a participant. In terrorist episodes especially, it frequently is the central nervous system for all the parties, brokering emotions, sometimes managing negotiations and performing all sorts of other services or disservices. In these conditions, television literally changes the course of events. It alters official positions. It affects outcomes.

Television executives claim their coverage frequently shortens crises and saves hostage lives. Most experts argue that the debits usually outrun the credits. What is not in dispute is that television is an active party in crises like Flight 847. Along with terrorists and governments, it is shaping events, helping to make history, not just reporting it. And whether television newsmen like it or not, this affects their position as journalists. When they are players on the field, they cannot also be standing on the sidelines in journalism's traditional pose of detached objectivity. Once again, this corrodes television's assertion of editorial license.

The people's "right to know," the battle cry of all reporters, was invented by the press, not the Founding Fathers, and loses validity altogether when it is exercised in the cause of celebrity journalism rather than in the national interest. Entertainment, drama, ego-puffing, and the mass production of emotion are nowhere listed as services essential to an informed society. Nor is frenzied competition, although it is honored in our capitalist tradition. So television journalism injures both the facts and itself when it sweeps all its acts under the cloak of public service. It is not the surrogate of the people, and it cannot exile itself from responsibility. It cannot claim immunity from outside restraint or coercion.

The issue is especially critical in the case of international terrorism, which has become an increasingly serious problem for the United States. During 1985, 926 people were killed and another 1,297 wounded in terrorist incidents around the world, far more victims than the year before and the worst wave of carnage since the State Department started keeping records in 1968. The attacks continued on into 1986 with the United States again singled out as a major target. Ironically, in March four Americans were killed by a bomb while flying to Athens on TWA Flight 840, the companion of Flight 847, which was the center of the Beirut crisis nine months earlier. In this wanton warfare, the stakes are too high and the role of cameras and satellites too critical to let the coverage problems drift out to sea, somewhere between government censorship and unlimited freedom.

Whatever the conflicts in role or perspective, it is in the public interest to reduce the value of American television to bombers and hijackers. For this to happen, the challenge of terrorism, the problems it presents to democratic societies, and the distorting influence of television must be examined intensively, continuously, and even more important, with a sense of adventure that liberates thought from conventional arguments and hoary tradition, "the eternal yesterday" as Max Weber defined it.

Television in the age of satellites cannot be equated with newspapers born in the seventeenth century, its height measured by the length of old shadows. It is different not just in kind but in essence, and the cliches of the press do not necessarily apply. It has to be seen for what it is or will be; it has to develop its own relationship to society. Its behavior has to evolve from this relationship and from its own unique nature, with journalistic responsibility and performance matched to its special powers to excite and modify the life around us.

# 2 / Why Television Is So Different

Every night, television delivers the world into living rooms across the nation, putting ordinary viewers in vicarious contact with the great and near-great, with distant lands and strange peoples. Images swim by in endless profusion, fires and plane crashes, statesmen and mayors, controversy and violence, weather and sports. Visual impressions in numbing volume, immediate and global, existential and emotional. Feelings bypassing reason, leaving the mind untouched. Mass opinions formed, not in crowds or town halls or even over backyard fences but in individual reactions that are multiplied over and over until they become a force that moves leaders and changes policies—even defeats presidential candidates.

When the votes had all been counted in November 1984, Walter Mondale stood before the cameras for the last time in his campaign and formally surrendered the presidential election system to television. "Modern politics today requires a mastery of television," he said. "I've never really warmed up to television and, in fairness to television, it's never warmed up to me." Why he felt he should be fair to television was a puzzle, but he was right when he said: "I don't believe it's possible anymore to run for president without the capacity to build confidence and communications every night. It's got to be done that way"—as Reagan demonstrated with consummate skill.[1]

In a more recent confirmation of Mondale's point, it was television that delivered the final blows which drove President Ferdinand Marcos out of office. Those scenes of thousands of protesters with their yellow ribbons, blocking the path of armored cars, were devastating. Marcos with his pewter face and autocratic manner could not compete with Corazon Aquino's telegenic image, attractive, articulate, spunky. With American television crews smothering the story and international observers poking into every corner, Marcos could not control the coverage in his usual imperial way. During the military showdown at the end, he was not able even to hold his own national television stations. "When we lost Channel 4, we were in trouble," said an aide, and when Channel 9 fell, "we lost all the initiative."[2]

Television's impact on the Philippine voters was no surprise. But the effect on U.S. viewers was nothing less than stunning. The Philippines was once a U.S. territory and a center of struggle during World War II, but in 1986 it stood about as far away from ordinary American interests as anyone could imagine. Yet the network coverage was so compelling that for weeks the Philippine elections were a continuing national issue, debated in bars as well as in Congress and the White House. The elections were good television, a visual drama with a heroine and a villain, a case of good fighting evil, and suspense that kept everyone guessing until the American air force plane finally took off for Guam with its cargo of corruption and defeat. It was an achievement newspapers could not duplicate.

### Transmission of Experience

What sets television apart from all the other forms of communication ever invented is this ability to transmit actual experiences in a living, breathing, visual form. When a newspaper reporter writes a story it is already in the past tense. No matter how strongly he reacts to what he has seen—the bodies scattered on the terminal floor after the bombing at Rome's da Vinci Airport—he has to convert his impressions into words. It is an act of recollection and translation that dilutes emotions. When a newspaper publishes his story hours later, on gray pages with unmoving pictures, more time and space intervene between the original action and the reader's perceptions.

In the case of television, by contrast, the experience itself can be captured with all of its immediacy, motion, sound, and color and then delivered to viewers without translation or dilution. It is neither history nor the past; it is a vivid present transported instantly from a White House press conference or exploding bombs in Tripoli. It is a single event experienced by people in one area which is then relived by millions of people in many other areas.

Can anyone ever forget that moment last January 28 when the space shuttle *Challenger* arced up across the sky over the Atlantic and then suddenly disappeared in forked clouds of white gas? Or the shock that slowly spread through everyone when they realized they had just seen seven people die? Within minutes, a nation went into mourning without announcement or decree. It was an experience immediately felt by the millions who were watching when the explosion occurred, and shared by other millions in the United States and around the world as the plumes of death were shown again and again in thousands of broadcasts.

The tragedy dramatized something else that makes television unique. It is not only able to move actual experiences from place to place but it can repeat experiences at will. And this comes close to tinkering with our philosophies. The moon walk was extraordinary not so much for its technology or human valor but for its philosophy. For the first time in human existence, man stood on a distant perch, outside the only world he had ever known. Through the wonder of television, he stood with Neil Armstrong and Edwin Aldrin and looked down on his little globe and finally understood, in a way he never could before, that he was only a mote in the universe, not its center as earthbound tradition had taught. In a less cosmic but analogous way, television permits us for the first time to move experience from one time to another so that we can relive and rearrange life itself.

## How Pictures Lie

This is not to say that video experiences come to us in a pure and unaltered form. Not at all. In fact, with the exception of live coverage of events like the moon walk or a presidential inauguration, television always changes the reality it sees—and usually intensifies it. Nothing very sinister is intended. It is simply a matter of selection—taking samples from the "infinite flotsam" of events,[3] focusing tightly on what is most interesting, then putting everything together in a dramatic form. The result is that the television experience often differs considerably from the original. And contrary to myth, pictures do tell lies, mostly fibs and medium-sized white lies, but sometimes real whoppers.

Elaine Sciolino of The New York Times tells about the time she was covering the climax of the Iranian revolution for Newsweek. There were wild celebrations all over Tehran. The streets were crowded with people, cheering, dancing, and throwing flowers. She filed a color story with a festive spin to it and then dropped around to a television network bureau. She wanted a friend to show her the film they had, in case she had missed something. She had. There in the videotape was a correspondent doing a stand-up in front of a burning building and talking about turbulent waves of screaming revolutionaries. "It must have been the only burning building in Tehran," she said. "But it gave them the drama they wanted."⁴ The burning building was true; but the story told by the pictures was false.

Television always moves in close on its subjects to provide focus and impact. The result is that the camera concentrates on a face, the wreckage of a plane, protesters in front of an embassy gate. It seldom pulls back to show how its small vignettes fit into the larger murals of news, the general scene at a disaster, or the normal activity surrounding an act of violence. This is good dramatic technique but it distorts reality by robbing stories of context and perspective. So scenes of subway crime give people in other cities the idea that New Yorkers are living under siege, an impression that is now so pervasive some New Yorkers even believe it.

Close-ups do their finest work—and sometimes their worst—on personalities. The camera is a merciless reporter that reveals every worry line on a president's face, his every mannerism, his body language, his gestures. The microphone catches the words he says, the voice and intonation, every slip of the tongue or error in fact. Emotions, changing moods, and personal chemistry somehow find their way onto the screen and, out of it all, viewers make a judgment. In all the roles he has played, from the Gipper to president, Reagan comes across to millions as the nice guy next door. And, as White House correspondents confirm, the man on the screen is the same one his aides see in the Oval Office. It is one of the secrets of his great political power.

### Words for Defense

Television's profound overall impact on the presidency and on the entire democratic process is a separate issue now being studied by Cyrus Vance and others. But one of the keys to the phenomenon, certainly, is this ability of television to draw personal portraits of public figures and to imprint them on millions of minds on a scale and with a mass intensity that is beyond the reach of words. Imagination is being ruined in the process, of course, and written language is threatened. Indeed, it is already disappearing in places like corporate boardrooms and the White House where the oral-visual cult prevails. In his kiss-and-tell book about his days as budget director, David A.

Stockman said the president's deputy chief of staff, Michael K. Deaver, and his White House colleagues "never read anything. They lived off the tube."[5]

This is lamentable because words are still the best defense we have against the lies that pictures can tell. They are the only way, for example, to explain that the shaven Nabih Berri was not only Olga Conwell's "friend" and a host at hostage dinners but the head of a militia that does a lot of killing off screen. We have seen tapes showing Yasir Arafat smiling, hugging babies, and looking for peace with Jordan's King Hussein, but never throwing any bombs. For the bombing activity, journalism has to turn to words, and they don't compete very well in an age when children are raised on sight and sound.

In *Crime and Punishment* we hear Raskolnikov cry out to Sonia, "I wanted to have the daring . . . and I killed her. I only wanted to have the daring, Sonia." In our imaginations we conjure up the man and a sense of what he was. We can be gripped as powerfully by what we do not see as we are by reality itself. The picture that appears in one mind may vary from the one that develops in another; both may clash with illustrations in the book or with scenes in the movie. Yet the paradox is that all the different Raskolnikovs are true, for there is a common, pervasive view of violence, evil, and guilt.

It is this point of view that is so often missing in the impassive work of the camera. The "in" word for this at the networks is "context." The message television delivers in the case of Reagan's personality or Richard Nixon's, in the coverage of *Challenger* or the Philippine elections, may be clearer and more accurate than even the most perceptive writing. But many times it misleads because the tape is not put into context. That lavish party the shah gave, which we all went to with Barbara Walters and television, turned out to be a Potemkin Village cutting off our view of the real Iran. The media's portrait of the shah, popular, progressive, man of vision, was a false front—which newspapers, incidentally, also did little to expose.

### Stereotypes Destroyed

The shah illustrates how television creates, changes, and manipulates the stereotypes with which we all live. From families, neighbors, newspapers, and a thousand other sources we develop mental indexes so we can put people into different cubbyholes for quick identification. These are colored by prejudice and myth, and sometimes can be very destructive. This has been true, for instance, with segregation in this country, the Pentagon's opinion of those peasant guerrillas in Vietnam, and the incredible idea that the Japanese could only make cheap toys. One of the sturdier stereotypes we have is that villains should always have bushy black beards and look fierce, but even they often get twisted out of shape by television.

Russian leaders are a case in point. They are all supposed to be a replay of a Stalin or at least a Leonid Brezhnev. Then along comes Mikhail S. Gorbachev looking like an investment banker, with a wife who is stylish instead of dumpy and, poof, the stereotype disappears. He is in charge of killing Afghans, sending arms to Cuba and Nicaragua, secretly helping Gaddafi, and doing all sorts of other uncharitable things. But the pictures show the smiling couple with Reagan at the summit and hobnobbing with Margaret Thatcher in London. So the public image of Gorbachev shifts from the old stereotype to an impression, as *Time* magazine put it, of a "handshaking, baby-kissing American politician."[6]

The stereotype of terrorists is upset in a similar way when television close-ups clash with ideas already stored away in the public mind. Americans used to expect all terrorists to have the menacing looks of a Che Guevara; now they think of Gaddafi, a masterwork that improves on earlier models. Those television shots of Gaddafi after the U.S. Sixth Fleet's show of force last March were superb. There he was, being carried on the shoulders of cheering Libyans, glaring triumphantly, waving his arms wildly, shouting rabble-rousing defiance, the very epitome of madness.

But in Beirut, television told a different tale. After that early picture of the gunman and pilot, we saw Berri looking like the lawyer that he is, reasonable rather than violent, and the hostages chatting and eating in a chummy restaurant setting. This may have lowered public fears and reduced pressures on the White House, as some officials concede, but television and reality were still out of joint. And after seeing the hostages paraded before a staged press conference, all the incongruities came to roost in *The New York Times's* John Corry's mind: "It was an obscene travesty of a news conference," he wrote, "serving no one other than the hijackers. Meanwhile, when we do see terrorists on television we are struck by their ordinariness. How can we deplore people who look very much like us?" Tom Shales of the *Washington Post* reached the same conclusion. "Television-age terrorism takes on the trappings of ordinariness and civility," he said. "During this crisis, television allowed terrorism to look like a mere alternate lifestyle."[7]

### Repetition of Experience

Television also does something else that readjusts reality and viewer responses to suit its unique needs. As mentioned before, it records experience and then calls it back to the screen in its original form. It does not simply refer to a past event, as newspapers are forced to do; it repeats the event itself. Instead of having to remember what they have seen before, viewers relive the experience, feel the same shock or the same anger. In times of high drama, tape is edited down to the bare essentials to highlight the most emotive moments and these are then repeated over and over. They pummel nervous systems and intensify reactions until sometimes the repetition itself changes history.

Haig, for example, admits that his days as secretary of state were cut short by his famous "I am in control" statement at the time of the assassination attempt on the president. What really did him in, he believes, was not the remark itself but the fact that the tape was tightly edited and played again and again, piling up criticism both inside and outside the White House. The gaffe might never have attracted attention if it had not been repeated almost hourly at a time of maximum public attention.

Mondale benefited briefly from the same technique when Reagan fumbled his thoughts during their first debate in the 1984 election campaign. The initial polls showed the public really hadn't noticed any flubs and felt the president had held his own. The networks, however, pounced on the issue and replayed the incriminating tapes over and over while all the commentators weighed in with ominous analyses. Sure enough, the public eventually realized its error and shifted back toward the television verdict. Once again, said the *Washington Post's* chief pollster Barry Sussman, television had displayed "its immense power to create, change or manipulate public opinion."[8]

What is true in American politics is true also in the coverage of terror. When news first breaks it is information the public should have, whether this helps or hurts the government. When the news is massaged for dramatic effect, heavily promoted, and repeated with breathless urgency on every network and local station, hour after hour, the original report changes character. It is converted from information to emotional hype, particularly when the repetition involves interviews with terrorists or hostages. It becomes a form of psychological conditioning like brainwashing. The result is that events are bent out of shape and governments are pressured into unwise decisions, adding to the world's already weighty burden of folly. "The most harmful effect of television news," says Lloyd Cutler, "is its tendency to speed up the decision-making process on issues that television news is featuring and to slow down and interrupt the process of deciding other important issues that get less television attention."[9]

All of these phenomena peculiar to television—the replication, transmission, and repetition of experience, the manipulation of images and personalities, the rearranging of events—contribute to a more general problem: a blurring of the line between the medium and the message, between substance and illusion, between the real and the unreal. When television leaves smiles on the faces of terror, when it stages or rearranges news for dramatic effect, when it mixes reporting with entertainment and links it to celebrity anchors, it is remaking reality in its own image. The result is the shadow on Plato's cave, something a person can see and hear and respond to emotionally but not touch, as he might touch a dented fender on his car after hitting a fence.

For all its power, the television image has a genetic defect. "Our eyes are accustomed to seeing a dilute reality on the screen," said Jack Rosenthal of The New York Times. "It is a distilled reality, but our eyes don't know how to distinguish and we become afraid of crime or affected by events in a highly intensified way which may or may not be real."[10] In life as in Othello, however, emotions based on illusion can be just as destructive as those that spring from fact, and this is television's burden. "We very often convey illusion to the viewer," ABC's Peter Jennings has observed. "We are constantly demanding that the viewer sift reality from image in the maelstrom which is television as a whole."[11] So in the end, the most powerful of all the media does not take up the burden. It is the individual who is expected to seek answers to the philosophers' ancient questions:

"What exists? What do I know? What is true?"

# 3 / Television in Captivity

Although news executives demand total freedom to report any and all terror, they exercise that freedom very selectively, covering many incidents with a great deal more zeal than others, and almost totally ignoring some of the bloodiest deeds of all time, from the slaughter of 300,000 Mao Communists in Indonesia to the "killing fields" in Cambodia. The decisive factors in coverage decisions are American involvement—how many Americans are trapped in the hijacked plane?—and the dramatic force of the story, the human anguish, the danger, the suspense. Critical to dramatic appeal, of course, is access, the ability to record the fear and suffering so that they can be reproduced for home use.

Terror in closed societies or far-off places, beyond the camera's red eye, is terror that does not exist for Americans, like the tree falling in the forest without a sound because no one is there to listen. When daring cameramen cover mujahadeen operations in the Afghan mountains, the campaign against Soviet troops exists for us. When there is no tape, that distant struggle disappears into a fog bank of other images being rushed into our heads.

The ebb and flow of public interests—shifting moods and attitudes—also influence coverage because television producers swim in the same pool as the public; they are subject to the same cultural biases, caught up in the same trends. Alexis de Tocqueville, one of history's greatest reporters, observed more than 140 years ago that "a newspaper can only subsist on the condition of publishing sentiments or principles common to a large number of men. A newspaper therefore always represents an association which is composed of its habitual readers."[1] Similarly, television newscasters belong to an association of viewers that is as large as society itself. So news fashions keep company with popular fashions and change with them. This is as true for terror as it is for politics or any other news.

Back in the 1930s when the Ku Klux Klan was conducting lynchings and committing other acts of terrorism against blacks, newspapers were deliberately inattentive. The ruling whites accepted the violence, and the general press, with a few notable exceptions, did not get very outraged. The same kind of social psychology prevailed when I first covered a police beat in Brooklyn immediately after World War II. It was unfashionable then to report acts of private terrorism or police brutality against blacks. The press simply accepted the social order in which blacks were only "cheap addresses," as my old city editor used to say. As a result, a great deal of domestic terrorism—mostly involving blacks—went totally unreported.

But everything changed later. In this country, the civil rights movement captured the nation's conscience and televised scenes of violence in places like Selma created a wave of revulsion against personal terror. The American press suddenly discovered the big city ghettos and, twenty years after I had worked in the Brooklyn "shacks," as the police reporters' hangout was called, attacks against blacks finally made the papers. Later on, during the Vietnam War years, riots and demonstrations spread like the flu and were covered massively, until the media finally got tired of being manipulated and, with public encouragement, turned off the klieg lights.

### Freedom Fighters

On the international front, meanwhile, journalistic attitudes toward terrorism were moving in a different direction. Terrorists were thought of as guerrillas, freedom fighters struggling against heavy odds and superior weapons to overthrow their Western colonial rulers. There were the Vietminh in French Indochina, the Irgun Zvi Leumi in Palestine, the Mau Mau in Kenya, the Front de Liberation Nationale (FLN) in Algeria. They were seen to be fighting for their independence as we had for ours nearly two centuries earlier, and this activated our revolutionary genes.

The mass media, riding the communications revolution to

ever-increasing power, happily gave the anticolonial movements a megaphone to mobilize support for their causes. Terrorism had respectability because it was helping destroy the old colonial world and relieving liberal democracies of their guilt. Guerrilla leaders were portrayed as heroes; white colonialists in places like Kenya, Southern Rhodesia, and the Congo were the villains. More important, the whole revolutionary tide was accelerated by the media's rapid transfer of information from one society to another.

Together with the transportation revolution, mass communications created new mass societies everywhere. These were not simply large; they were the sum of an enormous increase in individual interactions between people. The number of persons one came to know at least indirectly, the distant events that became a daily experience, multiplied exponentially so that, as Harvard's Daniel Bell observed, there was an unprecedented surge in "sociological density."[2] In the process, struggling new nations learned instantly what their neighbors had and they lacked, who was being exploited and who was not. Everyone was made personally conscious of contrasting lifestyles: the rich versus the poor, the haves versus the have-nots, the powerful versus the weak. People were more quickly aroused, therefore, about perceived wrongs, far more vocal, activist, and violent than before.

Communications technology gathered speed along with the social turmoil. Declining costs, the mass production of television sets, the invention of Minicams, satellite relays, and mobile ground stations extended television's reach into every corner of the earth, from the video parlors of Leh in Kashmir to the BOP television channel in Bophuthatswana. Cameramen, the front-line journalists in television, were no longer held on a short leash by heavy equipment or studio dependency. They could get to the scenes of disaster and violence with the ambulances. So the patterns of coverage changed, becoming more extensive than ever before—more immediate, more vivid, more global in their impact on people and events. Everywhere, relations between people and nations were altered in ways no one understood because, as usual, change was running ahead of knowledge, a fact that prompted T. S. Eliot's famous query:

Where is the wisdom we have lost in information?
Where is the knowledge we have lost in information?

For a number of reasons, including television's growing involvement, terrorism also changed. It developed new forms and new techniques, in different countries and at different times, until finally it became national policy in rogue states like Libya. Anticolonial struggles became entangled in the cold war; the Middle East was a collision of cultures and power. Along the way, the idealistic image of the freedom fighter became blurred; it never exactly died but it dimmed. American attitudes turned hostile as innocent civilians were wantonly killed or maimed, as U.S. diplomats, businessmen, and tourists came under attack. People were outraged by the Munich massacre of Israeli athletes. They instinctively opposed the terrorist assaults against our ally Israel, which they saw as a small, embattled democracy surrounded by autocratic and culturally alien regimes. They didn't quite know whom to back in Central America, but terrorism lost favor with the American public—just as advancing technology was helping terrorists exploit American television while they killed more American citizens.

### Stupefying Excess

All these trends came together with a crash in Beirut. All the issues that terrorism poses were joined there—the antagonism of interests, the tensions between cultures, the blinding emotions, the dilemmas of victims, governments, and journalism, and finally the inequality of advantages. Inequality because the captors, who held the hostages, were in a better position than anyone else to control events and make accomplices of the media.

Every fact in the crisis seemed to have different interpretations, every question several answers. On one issue, however, there was unanimous consent: television coverage had been carried to stupefying excess. Richard C. Wald, ABC's senior vice president of news and a former newspaper editor, conceded "the volume of reporting was so staggering that it became tasteless."[3] Other important news was swept to oblivion because of the networks' obsession with Flight 847. It was an orgy of overkill that exploited the hostages, their families, and the American people.

In a study he did at George Washington University, William C. Adams reported that the three networks had devoted a "staggering" 62 to 68 percent of their evening news shows to the hostage crisis.[4] On the second day of the crisis, when the story was really rolling, CBS carried thirteen special reports, plus expanded evening news coverage and numerous news bulletins and program break-ins.

CBS News Special Report, 8:07 a.m.:

RATHER: The nightmare . . . continues into day two . . .

WOMAN: Some of us heard the beatings. . . .

CBS News Bulletin, 11:01 a.m.:

RATHER: . . . This long day has seen the hijackers free roughly 70 of their prisoners. One is the mother of a young boy in Boston.

BOY: Now that she's off . . . I'm not scared any more. I'm gonna sleep all right . . .

ABC, which had a lock on exclusive interviews with the hostages, aired them for 37 percent of its news time. It devoted 13 percent of its coverage to the families and 15 percent to Nabih Berri and his media managers. Berri to ABC's Charles Glass: "I give guarantee to the American and to everyone, to the Greek, everyone, that nobody get hurt." Edwin Diamond and his News Study Group at New York University analyzed sixty hours logged by the three networks and found a polarized pattern of "individual journalistic achievement and collective news mindlessness." With the benefit of hindsight, he concluded that when all the parts were finally put together, "the TV system collectively went wrong" and the crisis had "transformed moderate television into terrorvision."[5]

It is customary to blame competition for ravenous assaults on the news. Many critics with zero-sum knowledge of the business assume that network newsmen are just chasing Neilsen ratings, sponsors, and money when they swarm over a story. Wrong. When a big story breaks, something quite different happens. Adrenalin surges. The entire nervous system mobilizes the body's resources. Every man and woman in the newsroom is instantly gripped by a single thought: "What a story!" Without a signal from anyone, the newsroom is convulsed. Writers crank out early bulletins which correspondents hurry onto the air while other people chase down background information and library tape. Producers are mobilizing their field forces: "Where the hell is Charlie Glass? Find Tom, he's in some jungle in Africa." They rush crews and equipment to planes, guess where to send them, worry about visas and security.

News executives, just as stimulated as their junior reporters, are meanwhile churning with ideas: "Go after the ambassador in Algiers, see what he knows. . . . Check the airline for a passenger list, we gotta track down the families, get stills of the hostages. . . . How can we get a shot of the plane? . . . Get on the horn to Julie, see if she can find out who's running the hijackers." In the first minutes and hours, the obsession is to blanket the story, cover every angle, get all the comment anyone can find, develop interviews and other sidebars. Someone is try ing to keep tabs on the competition but no one has time immediately to pay close attention. The dominant emotion is a compulsion to get the story and play it big.

## Out of Control

In the TWA case, the news centers were quickly awash with new developments, film, field reports, interviews, comments, and reactions. The general excitement spread to the corporate headquarters on Sixth Avenue. The news divisions were given a go-ahead to break in at will on network shows. News executives, always grieving about inadequate airtime, responded exuberantly. As the crisis progressed, competitive frenzy did take hold. The compulsion to be first with the most consumed everyone from Lebanon to New York. The lessons of the Iranian hostage days were lost somewhere in forgotten memos, and the story itself took charge. In many instances, as NBC's John Chancellor has noted, the networks simply lost control.[6]

Not only was the volume of coverage at the three networks enormous, but the cumulative impact was multiplied many times by Cable News Network, which was running continuously; by hundreds of local stations that crowded their own news shows with TWA developments; and also by radio and newspapers which, incidentally, were picking up much of their spot news from their television screens. "It's a television event," said James McCartney of the *Philadelphia Inquirer.* "Look at Berri. Is he talking to the *Washington Post, The New York Times* and the *Philadelphia Inquirer?* No, he's calling the networks."[7]

When all was said and done, the networks concluded that the blizzard of bulletins and special reports was simply too much and that the total effect was "tasteless," particularly the incessant interviewing of hostages' families. The families themselves often seek television coverage to focus attention on the plight of their loved ones; but when carried to excess the interviews not only invade people's privacy, they overheat popular feelings and finally put undue pressure on the government. Katharine

Graham of the *Washington Post* said, "There is real danger that public opinion can be unjustifiably influenced by exposure to the hostage relatives and wives"[8]—including that part of public opinion which is the president.

### Reagan a Viewer Too

When Israel invaded Lebanon in 1982, Reagan was appalled by the graphic scenes of killing and destruction that he saw on television. Once the attack had begun, former Secretary of State Haig said it was in America's interest for Israel to succeed in routing the PLO. But, he said, "the president was so deeply impressed by what he saw that he phoned Prime Minister Menachem Begin requesting a halt to the bombing."[9] Television again played on the president's feelings when the Flight 847 story broke. During a special Sunday meeting on the crisis, he showed he was just as affected by the hostages' plight as any other viewer. As a result, a staffer confided later, it took more than an hour of strenuous argument, mainly by Secretary of State George Shultz, to persuade him to suppress his feelings about the hostages and hang tough publicly against any concessions to the terrorists.

Whether the administration later retreated is argued several ways. What is certain is that massed emotions centered on hostages and families can bend policy in a direction that is different from what a president intends. Among other things, it absolutely rules out immediate military action because of the human risks. And because this fact is always well advertised, mainly by the media, the credibility of military threats is also undermined. An attempt to rescue this credibility was said to have been one objective last spring when the president sent the U.S. Sixth Fleet into the Gulf of Sidra to provoke a clash with Gaddafi—starting the chain of events that led to the bombing of a West Berlin discotheque and later to the American retaliatory air raid against Libya.

A related issue in terrorist crises is how the media can report what is essential without revealing information that risks lives, interferes with government actions, or damages national security. The problem cropped up the very first night of the TWA story when Roger Mudd was anchoring the "Nightly News" in the absence of the pith-helmeted Brokaw. Well into the broadcast, he turned to his man at the Pentagon, Fred Francis, and asked what the United States might do if the hostage negotiations failed. Francis immediately showed he had been working. "NBC learned this afternoon," he said, "that the anti-terrorist unit, Delta Force, did leave Pope Air Force Base in the Carolinas this afternoon heading for the Mediterranean." ABC carried the report later, but CBS said it held off for two days. The Associated Press withheld the news for security reasons until after NBC made it public property.

Wald said ABC went with the story because the existence and purpose of Delta were well known and it would be expected to be involved in the crisis. He also said a colonel had told their Pentagon reporter about Delta's movement "on a background basis," meaning the information could be used as long as it was not attributed to the Defense Department. ABC immediately assumed they were being handed a leak.[10] Lawrence K. Grossman, president of NBC News, said, "This is exactly what happened." I could identify with that, having wallowed in leaks myself during fifteen years' service as a Washington correspondent. It is the quaint way American officials have of communicating with each other and with governments. It would be natural to conclude that the Delta leak was intentional, an unofficial warning to the terrorists.

### Hijackers Warned?

On investigation, however, it turns out it actually was a gnashed bureaucratic gear, also a common occurrence in the machinery of government. Robert B. Oakley, ambassador-at-large for counter-terrorism, said everyone at the top of the administration, including the White House, had ordered the Delta moves held under heavy wraps. The reason was compelling. At all costs, they wanted to keep the hostage plane in Algiers where there was a more reasonable government to deal with. They had gotten a Red Cross negotiating team aboard and were hoping for a breakthrough.[11]

At about midnight Saturday, June 15, the gunmen said nothing else would happen during the night and the negotiators left to get some sleep. Later, however, the hijackers suddenly switched signals, forced the plane to take off, and flew with their remaining hostages to Beirut. Although network correspondents question whether the Delta report ever reached the plane, Oakley and others in the government claim they have evidence the terrorists were spooked by it. Shultz himself says the media "probably caused" the collapse of the Algiers negotiations and the shift of the crisis to the Amal's lair in Lebanon.[12] Said the Pentagon's former spokesman, Michael I. Burch: "For the price of a 25-cent newspaper or a 19-inch television screen, these hijackers had a very sophisticated intelligence system."

On another occasion, the navy had to scramble an F-14 Tomcat to chase a plane away from a U.S. flotilla that had been ordered in close to Lebanon. It was not a Syrian spycraft; it was a plane hired by CBS to take pictures that later showed American audiences how the navy had arrived at the scene of crisis. As John Dillin of the *Christian Science Monitor* reported, "anyone with a TV could learn the Navy had dispatched the carrier *Nimitz* with more than 90 planes aboard to Lebanon's coast." He said CBS also supplied the helpful information that the fleet included an amphibious task force with tanks, helicopters, and 1,800 marines. The disclosures were followed by a reporter's Format A defense: "It's ridiculous to believe that the Amal didn't know that a whole fleet was steaming around 30 miles off the coast."

Maybe yes, maybe no. But the terrorists were very jumpy. They were rattled by rumors of an air raid, by the sound of gunfire from an Israeli patrol boat offshore, and by a local radio report of a marine helicopter flying in from Cyprus. Whatever alarmed them, they suddenly herded all the press away from the airport one night and, except for the TWA crew, smuggled the hostages out to hideouts less accessible to any rescue mission. Officials cannot prove the fleet reports triggered the action, but neither can the media prove they did not.

### Media Responsibility

As evidence of responsible journalism, the networks all cite the fact that they never revealed the identities of three TWA passengers with sensitive government jobs, including an employee of the National Security Agency. True enough. It is also true that reporters really do not want to reveal military secrets that would jeopardize national security. "It isn't just hard to be against national security; it's inconceivable," said the *Washington Post*'s executive editor, Benjamin C. Bradlee.[13] The Delta leak began with a Pentagon source and a fleet cannot hide in a tent, so there were ambiguities—NBC and CBS decided one way, AP another. But when journalists insist on making the judgment calls themselves, even when lives are involved and government is supposed to be in charge, they bear responsibility for the consequences, whether it is the hiding of hostages from would-be rescuers or something worse. As one television executive told Katharine Graham: "Errors that threaten loss of life are permanent; others are temporary. If we have to make mistakes, we want to make the temporary kind."[14]

Some permanent mistakes have been made, nevertheless. In April 1983, sixty-three people were killed when terrorists bombed the American embassy in Beirut. At the time, the United States was able to link the atrocity to Syria and Iran because it had been intercepting the coded traffic between them. This critical source of information was cut off abruptly, however, after a television network and a newspaper columnist exposed the intelligence operation. The following October, terrorists believed to be the same as those who hit the embassy blew up the marine barracks, killing 241. There were no coded messages giving the authorities any advance warning, only silence until the bombs exploded.

One was reminded of this after the Berlin discotheque bombing in April 1986. Newspapers reported that evidence of a Libyan connection was so sensitive the United States could only secretly share it with a few allies. They then confided their belief that the information included intercepted and decoded messages from Libya as well as phone tap and surveillance intelligence.

In the fall of 1985, Egyptian commandos were flying into Malta to storm a hijacked EgyptAir jet. Ambassador Oakley remembers seeing television pictures of the plane's approach and a correspondent explaining its supposedly secret mission. In the gun battle that followed, fifty-seven people on the airliner died. No one knows whether the television report alerted the terrorists, but Oakley believes it was possible. During the Iranian hostage crisis, Carter secretly planned to send an emissary to Iran. The press got wind of what was happening, and according to Jody Powell, reporters went directly to Khomeini and asked whether he would talk to a Carter representative. In the glare of publicity, the Ayatollah said no. During the 1977 hijacking of a Lufthansa jetliner to Somalia, the media broadcast the fact that the pilot was radioing information to the police. The terrorists heard the news report and executed the pilot. Later, when West German commandos launched a rescue mission, local Israeli television announced the operation several hours in advance. At Israel's request, the wire services and Israeli radio agreed not to relay the report. Otherwise, said author Neil Livingstone, "it could have compromised the whole affair."[15]

### Need to Know

In incidents like these, the media's loose management of sensitive information is indefensible. There are good reasons not to allow the government to dictate what may be published in a free society, hence the rights that the press enjoys under the First Amendment. These rights are lodged in the Constitution, but the press draws its authority from the people. Everything the press does, as it says so often, is justified by the public's "need to know." And it is this "need" that is the crux of the security issue. For it is easy to claim the public has a "right" to know where its Delta Force is traveling; it is not so easy to claim it has a "need" to know. And it is impossible to argue that the public has to have the news instantly, in the middle of terrorist negotiations, when the real motive for rushing on the air is competition.

This immediacy is one of the qualities that distinguishes television from newspapers. Television has the ability to deliver news to its clients instantly, from any quarter of the earth. Newspapers have to convert news into words, printing plates, and newsprint; they then have to deliver it in slow-moving trucks so that it arrives hours after people have already heard the headlines and seen the pictures on television. The difference between these two information systems has had a profound effect on everything from social patterns and the democratic process in this country to a storm of change elsewhere in the world. It is so basic it even alters life's rhythms, for it is communication that explains why change is slow in rural China and life is frenetic in New York City. According to the experts, it also helps explain the explosive increase in modern terrorism, which operates mainly in urban centers where there are media, cars, and planes, as well as large supplies of targets.

Because of its immediacy, television pushes life into fast forward—and civilization into reverse? It sends images on and off the mind's screen so rapidly and in such profusion that it subtly changes the nature of knowledge itself; instant feelings and impressions crowd out the reflective reasoning on which wisdom depends. News operations move at a faster clip even than those of the wire services, which still cannot cover an event live. The whole culture of the television newsroom, therefore, is geared toward immediate action and superficial treatment. It eliminates, as the late Theodore H. White wrote, "the filter of time, the pause for reflection."[16]

In the coverage of terrorism, said columnist Charles Krauthammer, the problem is to fix on the subject of evil "without merging with it." For many arts, he said, "the solution is to interpose time: their reflections on evil are, for the most part, recollections in tranquility. On television news, that protective distance disappears."[17] The lack of time's protection was an important factor in the misdeeds charged against television in Beirut—leaking military secrets, negotiating, staging events, interviewing terrorists live, airing raw footage without editing, exploiting hostages, and paying families for exclusives. Immediacy, however, is a by-product of technology, not a journalistic imperative. Therefore, the risks it creates in terrorist incidents cannot be justified by the public's so-called need to know. They are the media's responsibility alone.

### Terror and Publicity

The emotional force driving all of the criticism is a pervasive national outrage over atrocities being committed against Americans for reasons people do not understand. Joined with this is the feeling that massive publicity is encouraging even more violence and that television, in particular, is giving terrorists a platform they should not have to promote their causes and to blackmail the United States.

On the publicity issue, all the authorities seem to agree. As long ago as 1976, the Justice Department's Task Force on Disorders and Terrorism concluded that "in many ways, the modern terrorist is the very creation of the media."[18] Ambassador Oakley, Neil Livingstone, Terrell E. Arnold, State Department consultant on terrorism, and many others are convinced that massive media coverage is a significant factor in the recent and continuing upsurge in international terrorism. In his excellent *The War Against Terrorism,* Livingstone noted that throughout history terrorists have used pamphlets, leaflets, and other techniques to send messages to the public. But with the development of mass societies and television's coming to power, they no longer could do this themselves; the printing press could not compete with the tube. They had to get professional help.

"In view of the inability of most terrorist organizations to disseminate their message through conventional mass media outlets," said Livingstone, "terrorists have sought instead to create news in order to communicate their existence, ideas, and power to the general public, cognizant that established news organizations will report their actions and deeds for them. Terrorists no longer need actually to grind out the propaganda; instead, all they have to do is produce an event and the news media will do the rest."[19] In other words, modern terrorism is a shotgun wedding that marries violent spectaculars to spectacular technologies.

Walter Laqueur sums up the thinking of many experts with the axiom: "The terrorist act alone is nothing, publicity is all." But this is an oversimplification that intense emotions tend to convert into a general truth, particularly where the Middle East is involved. It is dangerous because it misleads the public into thinking that all incidents of terror are just publicity stunts staged by mad glory-seekers like Gaddafi. The fact is otherwise, whether we like it or not. Actual grievances are often the chief motive, and understanding this is as important to the work of counter-terror as understanding the media's role. For example, the "forgotten" six Americans still held hostage in Lebanon in mid-1986 were so hidden away from cameras that no one could even be sure they were all alive. Their captors, who would not identify themselves, were quietly demanding freedom for prisoners held by Kuwait; the only calls for publicity came from the hostage families and Jerry Levin of Cable News Network, a fellow hostage who had escaped in 1985.

The networks could hardly muster a camera crew on the spot when the TWA hijackers finally set their crisis down in Beirut; the city had been abandoned by American news organizations. It was only after the media invaders began arriving in force that Berri and his aides took over public relations for the gunmen and helped produce a television extravaganza. Walter Mears, AP's executive editor in New York, was especially impressed by Berri's effort to make tapes and interviews equally available through pooling. "When Amal understands the pool system," he exclaimed, "that blows my mind. These guys are street fighters and they're making ground rules for the media."[20]

## Television Blackmail

The main objective of the TWA hijacking, as all the networks tried to make clear with varying degrees of success, was not publicity; it was blackmail. It was an attempt to force America to pressure Israel into releasing 766 Shiites who had been seized in Lebanon and were being held prisoner at Atlit, once a clandestine refuge for Jews fleeing Nazi Germany. The United States was the obvious target because everyone assumes it can tell its allies what to do. But the Shiites had a second reason, which the networks did little to explain and most Americans did not understand. To the Shiites, the United States became an enemy in 1983 when it unwittingly committed marines and naval guns on the side of the Christian Phalangists in the power struggle with Lebanon's Muslim majority.

## Shiites Tell Their Own Story

The three networks provided short bursts of background on the internal politics of the crisis with the help of assorted experts, ranging from academics like Fouad Ajami of Johns Hopkins, Peter Awn of Columbia, and Clinton Bailey of Tel Aviv University to Israeli officials and Lebanese and Iranian ambassadors. Even the Arab-American Anti-Discrimination Committee was given a hearing on "Nightline." The Shiites, however, told their own story better than all the anchors and experts put together—and on national television:

SHIITE WOMAN: I hope all of those who are away from home will be returned to their families, our children from Israel and the Americans to theirs.

It was a human message no slick commercial could match. And there were other messages like it. During an Amal-sponsored press conference, under guard, the leader of the American hostages, Allyn Conwell, said, "We understand that Israel is holding as hostage a number of Lebanese people who undoubtedly have as equal a right and as strong a desire to go home as we do." In his negotiations with Rather, Berri exuded reasonableness when he offered to exchange the Americans for the Shiite prisoners. As The New York Times's critic John Corry said later, "We had the feeling a bargain had been struck. Mr. Rather had not exactly obtained the release of the hostages, but he had told us how it could be done. . . . When Mr. Rather interviewed Mr. Berri, he was not a reporter; celebrity status made him a policy maker."[21]

The on-screen negotiations, the coverage of Shiite families, the airing of terrorist views, and the gun-covered statements of hostages—all this raised public temperatures. It also apparently changed attitudes, temporarily lowering Israel's approval rating, for example. One network poll showed a majority of Americans in favor of negotiations even though the president was opposed; 60 percent felt Israel should act itself to release its Shiite prisoners. Along with the poll results came heavy criticism. The networks were accused of flooding the nation with excuses for terrorists who had killed and kidnapped Americans and with propaganda for their cause. Fred Barnes, writing in the New Republic, said the Amal had been able to put their own "spin" on the story to a degree that was "beyond the wildest dreams of any politician."[22] Beneath the emotionalism, however, were fundamental journalistic issues.

# 4 / Television, Terror, and Policy

One fundamental issue highlighted by the TWA case is the question of moral equivalence, the idea that the network coverage as it swirled along tended to equate the kidnapping of 40 American hostages with Israel's abduction of 766 Shiites, implying collective guilt for a grievance with which America was not connected and overlooking the murder and violation of innocent American travelers. "The idea that seems to underlie some media coverage of terrorism," said George Will, "is this: Politics is a kind of physics, a field force. Journalists should maintain a physicist's detachment, a sophistication too languid for moral judgments. . . . It may be that one reason terrorists can so effectively use the media is the systematic, almost philosophic, proud, and even militant irresponsibility of the media."[1]

Lord Chalfont, author, journalist, and former British minister, observed at a conference on international terrorism in Jerusalem that television lets terrorists "disseminate their violent propaganda with the same freedom as a candidate for Parliament addressing his constituency." The problem, he said, stems from "some kind of bogus intellectual objectivity" that regards "the terrorist on the one hand and the policeman or the soldier on the other as two sides of a morally symmetrical confrontation."[2]

Objectivity is indeed the clue. In moderation it is sometimes useful but when it is a journalistic obsession, in form if not substance, it can be very damaging. Although prejudice has its faults, the cult of objectivity is more subversive because it also destroys truth on a fearful scale but does it in disguise. I remember a meatpackers' strike one time in which the union claimed and the company denied that it had set up housekeeping in the plant for scabs. Young and innocent in the ways of objectivity, I smuggled myself through a barbed wire fence and counted 125 beds. My editor refused to pay for the clothes I tore and rejected my exclusive on the ground that we had no spokesman to quote. Truth did not matter so long as the forms of impartiality had been observed.

The objectivity cult has changed over the years. Reporters now have ways of revealing their points of view while appearing to be frightfully detached and the "big feet" in television can influence viewers with a mere shrug or frown. But the old habits linger so that reporters are still running around looking for equivalence, automatically rounding up "the other side" of every issue, even when there is no other side worth mentioning. If one astronomer says the sun rises in the East, get another expert to say it rises in the West—that is the proper procedure. This custom is especially pernicious because it links artificial objectivity to our adversarial system, which is based on Milton's romantic myth that truth always wins out in any contest with falsehood. This overlooks the fact that falsehood often reigns for years— sometimes centuries as with the flat earth idea—before it is defeated. But the adversarial imperative does create controversy and that is something journalism likes even more than truth.

### Reagan vs. Radio Moscow

An illustration of applied equivalence was ABC's performance when President Reagan addressed the nation on military spending in February 1986. As it happened, Peter Jennings and cast were doing their show from Moscow the same night, and, sure enough, the "both-sides" reflex was so strong that a Russian propagandist was invited to join in the network's post-mortem on the speech. In a session with David Brinkley, Radio Moscow's Vladimir Posner spent an incredible eight minutes attacking the president's statements. When the White House protested, Richard Wald conceded ABC had given Posner "too much scope" because of a "production error." But, he said, "there is nothing wrong" in asking a Russian spokesman to comment on a presidential speech where U.S.-Soviet issues are involved. "It is part of what we do," he explained.

There is an essential flaw, however, in seeking balance in a wobbly world where there is no balance. If journalists really are looking for truth as they claim, they have to seek imbalance where that exists; searching out opposing comments and even actions to achieve journalistic symmetry is to distort what is real. In the very act of seeking rebuttal comments like Posner's, reporters often create conflicts that did not exist before and therefore substitute their own new reality for the old. The result, as Daniel Boorstin has observed, is that "synthetic happenings" replace "spontaneous events" and "a larger and larger proportion of our experience, of what we read and hear, has come to consist of psuedo-events."[3]

In Beirut, the whole news culture steered the coverage into familiar channels. The media rounded up hostage statements and family interviews, Berri proposals and White House reactions just as they always do—all the opposing views assembled for public review with the usual moral indifference required by objectivity. The problem is that opposing views tend to dominate when gunmen hold hostages and their staged events are dramatic. Richard Clutterbuck, a British authority on violence and subversion, once said, "The television camera is like a weapon lying in the street. Either side can pick it up and use it."[4] When terrorists use it, they shoot one way, and then journalism produces imbalance in the name of objectivity. It is another example of an ideal betrayed by its servant, the faithful representation of reality frustrated by news practices that distort and exaggerate reality. It is a case where imbalanced reporting could move journalism closer to truth.

### Information and Sensation

There is a significant difference between the information that a free society needs and a massive outpouring of emotionalized coverage controlled largely by hijackers. The networks certainly were right to provide "context and perspective" about the Shiites even though this conflicted with American stereotypes and therefore invited charges of propaganda. It is useful to distinguish between Amal grievances, which are specific, and the irrational acts of Gaddafi or, during an earlier period, the confused ideas of the Weathermen. But there is no need to air everything the terrorists offer just because it is available; even the old equal time rule would not require staged interviews that grossly exceed public need. At CBS, Rather personally ruled against using tapes of hostages speaking under terrorist control, but they were broadcast anyway.[5] More than his colleagues, Rather was also vigilant in warning viewers about the duress the hostages were under, use of tapes supplied by the terrorists, and other factors that might be misleading. But in the end, disclaimers were lost in the tide of drama. The cumulative effect of all the coverage was to load the dice in favor of the kidnappers.

Lawrence Grossman, president of NBC News, says there is "no evidence that audiences are ever taken in by the propaganda of terrorists."[6] In the sense of viewers siding with terrorists and against American hostages, this is true; no deserters were captured. Also, the mid-crisis polls showing a shift in attitudes against Israel are inconclusive. Nevertheless, it is clear that Americans did get a different view of the Shiites and the Amal than they ever had before. In many cases, television may reinforce the image of terrorists as thugs, as ABC's Richard Wald and some others argue, by stripping away their mystery and showing them as they really are. In Beirut, however, Berri signaled millions of viewers that all Muslim militants do not look like Gaddafi or Yasir Arafat and that some at least have definable grievances to which audiences can relate. The Amal used journalism's own pretensions of objectivity and equivalence to humanize their cause in a way that promoted understanding if not sympathy. They effectively manipulated the media.

### Manipulation by Terrorists

Television executives are the first to admit they are manipulated by terrorists. "Television has unquestionably become a primary vehicle for terrorists in search of an audience," said Grossman. "Television coverage gives terrorists status; it enables them, at least briefly, to transcend their underdog role ....They write the script for the opening act. They set the news agenda. Through television, they appeal directly to the people over the heads of the government. As the Rand Corporation's Brian Jenkins has said, 'Terrorists want a lot of people watching and listening; not a lot of people dead.'" Like cars and airplanes, Grossman concluded, television is a favorite tool of terrorists. "We have no choice but to learn to live with them and adapt to them."[7]

When the issue of manipulation is raised, television newsmen often have another curious response. They shrug and say, "Yes, the terrorists manipulate us. But everybody manipulates us. The White House does it all the time." This is the equivalence syndrome again. Setting aside the implications of manipulated information, what is striking about the argument is that it equates terrorists with presidents in the rubric of journalistic practice. Presidents certainly do a lot of manipulating, even in the case of terrorism. During the Iranian hostage crisis in 1980, the Carter White House made a deliberate political decision to pour on the publicity so that voters would be drawn to the president in shared sympathy and concern. Day after day, Jody Powell at the White House and Hodding Carter at the State Department made news even if there was none, and the media were fully cooperative. "That was the dumbest thing I ever did," Hodding Carter says now. "It was just plain stupid." He even congratulated ABC on the "America Held Hostage" slogan that drew so much criticism later. "But in terms of Jimmy's politics," Hodding Carter said, "the public diplomacy protected him all through the presidential primaries."[8]

In 1981, the Reagan media management corps took over under David Gergen, determined not to repeat Jimmy Carter's mistakes. The initial strategy was to get all the media to concentrate only on the administration's priority issue, "economic recovery." The project was moving along beautifully until, suddenly, Haig sent the media running off in a different direction with testimony about gun-running in Nicaragua. "The presidential ratings started slipping," Gergen recalls, "so we told Haig to get off TV." The secretary complained about neglecting a grave international threat but yielded. The television lights then swiveled around again to the White House.[9]

### Television Helps the White House

During the TWA crisis, the White House made heavy use of television, both as an information center and as a messenger. More than the public would ever dream, the U.S. government depends on the media in emergencies for information and even intelligence. Immediately after Egypt's President Anwar Sadat was shot in 1981, officials hovered over a television set in the White House situation room watching CNN's running coverage. Gergen said, "We had shut down any comment until the Egyptian government said Sadat had actually died. But we literally didn't know what was happening from minute to minute, even though we had an open telephone line to the embassy. The networks were so far ahead it was embarrassing. Everyone thought we were sitting on a lot of information or lying, but the fact was the networks knew a lot more than we did."[10]

The pattern was the same in Beirut; both sides used national television to exchange information and conduct business. Although the United States had a highly trained ambassador on duty in Lebanon, Berri preferred to do his talking on camera and presented his demands in television interviews. Reagan used television to reply: the United States would not be pressured; it would not demand that Israel release its Shiite prisoners. When negotiations bogged down, the White House passed the word that the president's patience was wearing thin. At another point, it encouraged media speculation that the United States might close the Beirut airport. And it joined the Amal and Israel in a "kabuki dance" around the Shiite prisoner issue, as former diplomat Lawrence Eagleburger put it—in a television interview, naturally.

Since the networks are already being manipulated by everyone else, one would think they could indulge in a little manipulation themselves without much further loss of integrity. They could, for instance, eliminate on-camera interviews with terrorists and only run enough tape on hostages to do two things: show their condition and deter captors from killing them. The problem is that coverage is controlled by competition and journalistic reflexes that do not discriminate greatly between a shoot-out in Miami and a complex international crisis. Stand-ups at a Lebanese restaurant are conducted much the same way as stand-ups near those flags in the State Department lobby. Man-in-the-street interviews when the *Achille Lauro* was hijacked looked just like those following a City Hall scandal. "Sir, do you think the president should use force to free those hostages?" The dramatic imperative in television is to humanize and personalize every story, no matter what the subject. When there is a Berri or an Arafat to focus on, the whole compulsion is to use more tape, not less. Even more than public need, therefore, journalistic techniques drive much of the publicity that both promotes terrorists and encourages terrorism.

### Arafat Primps for Television

There is no question that most terrorist leaders are fond of publicity, even those who, for reasons of security, have to stay in hiding. Mohammad Abbas, wanted for the *Achille Lauro* hijacking and the murder of one of its passengers, risked exposure and possible capture just to get an interview on NBC's "Nightly News." His controversial appearance, for which NBC was roundly criticized, represented personal power, psychic tonic, and most important perhaps, self-identification. "Television is a world stage and everyone wants to be on it," Neil Livingstone says, "to project themselves or their ideas through its magic, as if that were the only test of one's existence: I am on television, therefore I am."[11] So a man like Arafat is a familiar figure to millions, always seen basking in media attention and Israeli denuciations while his darker world remains hidden from the camera.

Like any other politician or television star, Arafat is acutely conscious of the importance of television to his persona; he may even think occasionally of its value to his cause. He likes to provide photo opportunities, under controlled conditions. It is simply astonishing how many times he is seen with a smile on his face, looking peaceful and benign, electronic image and reality at odds with each other again. He works constantly on his personal performance. With effort, he has improved his English and become eager for interviews with the Western media. He had media specialists coaching him on techniques and tactics to get a better press. "He has toned down his delivery," Livingstone says, "and eliminated most of the bombastic and obviously self-serving statements he used to make. His performances, consequently, are lower key with fewer extravagant gestures that might be appropriate before large crowds but that do not come across well on television."[12]

His looks, however, are a media disaster. Former Secretary of State William Rogers once remarked that Arafat needed a tailor. What he needs even more for American tastes is a face-lift and a personality change because on these points he just cannot compete with someone like Berri. He could never sell used cars to Americans, which allows broadcasters to argue that television, whatever its excesses, exposes terrorists for what they are. Grossman of NBC notes that "the most vivid picture to emerge from the TWA crisis" was the hooded terrorist with a pistol holding his hand over the pilot's mouth. Polls, he says, indicate increased public hostility toward terrorism. Wald of ABC insists that television actually strips the mystery away from terrorists and exposes their brutish nature.[13]

These analyses argue the case on the basis of American reactions, as if these were the only ones that mattered. This strong, ethnocentric view of the world, tracing back to our continental character and frontier origins, is a national flaw that affects nearly all we do, our foreign policy as well as our journalism, and explains much of the folly we commit. The narrowcasting of history and news uses American experience as the reference point for the world; this cuts us off from the experiences of other cultures. We then do not understand them, and we are surprised by what they do in Vietnam or Iran or Egypt, where a president lionized by the U.S. media was assassinated. And the same is true in Lebanon, where U.S. policy is ambushed and marines killed because we do not even know it when we take sides in a civil war.

In the case of terrorists, American reactions to their television performances often are less important than the responses of their own constituents. To be sure, terrorist leaders want to influence U.S. public opinion in order to pressure the president into doing what they want. But even if they fail in this, their televised defiance of the enemy makes them look like heroes to their followers. The same television personality that repels Americans may be very appealing to an Arab audience and therefore a source of personal prestige and political power. NBC's John Chancellor says this was the case during the Iranian hostage crisis. Sadegh Gotzbadegh, the Ayatollah's spokesman at the time, told him that "you TV people have it all mixed up; we were putting out the pictures to confirm the power of the revolution to our own people." There were a lot of television sets in Iran, Chancellor explains, and "in the beginning at least they were staging TV events for internal political reasons. The American aspect was secondary."[14]

### The "Contagion Factor"

In addition to serving the personal purposes of terrorist leaders, television does something else that is unrelated to the reactions of American audiences: it acts as a terror stimulant because its graphic coverage invites imitation. This is called the "copycatting effect" or "contagion factor." It is the phenomenon, familiar to every newsman, in which a highly publicized violent act is quickly followed by similar incidents, so terrorist events tend to occur in clusters. Clutterbuck says "ideas travel ...through the normal news media...people watching and listening to the reports get ideas about doing the same things themselves." Grossman concedes "the very existence of television undoubtedly bears some responsibility for the 'copycat' syndrome of terrorism today. News travels instantaneously from one end of the world to the other. One highly visible action inspires others elsewhere."[15]

## Television Fiction

The contagion effect is also multiplied by television drama that produces its own violence in large quantities. This is so skillfully blended with news that it is sometimes difficult to remember whether a gory scene came from "Miami Vice" or the evening news. And imitation follows television fiction as well as television news. In Boston a few years ago, a gang of youths set a young woman ablaze and watched her die after seeing the same thing happen on a television show. "It is art that makes life," said Henry James. So news and fiction follow each other in a circle until they arrive in the same place, yet another example of the circle theory of human behavior. "Television turns everything into television," says *Washington Post* critic Tom Shales. "It denatures events, even tragedies. . . . One week a jokey, campy massacre on 'Dynasty,' a few weeks later news film of a real massacre on a network newscast. It's hard to keep one's bearings in videoland."[16] The industry, however, likes to put everything into separate compartments, news in one cubbyhole, entertainment in another. It never thinks too much about the connection between the two. And whereas executives boast that commercials sell beer and automobiles, they insist television does not sell violence.

In 1982, the National Institute of Mental Health found a "causal relationship between television violence and real-life violence."[17] Surveying twenty-five years of research in 1980, John P. Murray concluded that "there is a relationship between violence on television and violence in society." During congressional testimony in 1984, he said a long-term study begun by CBS showed "an impressive relationship between violence viewing at age 8 and criminal behavior through age 30."[18] But the behavioral sciences are still immature and inexact. Much of the violence research is only short-range and focused on individual reactions; long-term social reactions are not well understood. Some experts conclude that television violence is strongly stimulative; others say it vicariously releases aggressive pressures—Aristotle's catharsis of emotion.

Whatever answers research finally supplies, there is persuasive empiric evidence for at least some of the stimulative effects of television news: It enhances the position of terrorist leaders and groups and it invites imitation that increases the incidence of violent acts. Most important of all, it creates powerful national emotions that fall heavily on government leaders and distort the democratic process by which decisions are made.

### Television Changes Democracy

When democracies set people free from kings, they made public opinion their ruler. But forming, organizing, and applying this opinion was a challenging proposition resolved, in the case of the United States, by representative democracy. Americans relied on newspapers for knowledge of the world beyond their home and work and exercised their political power indirectly through elected representatives who were presumed to be more experienced and better informed. This was the design of the Founding Fathers and essentially the way the system worked for 170 years—until television and the mass communications revolution. This momentous development, together with other social, technical, and economic changes, profoundly affected the whole democratic process. Among other things, it helped provoke egalitarian demands that led to the revolution of rising entitlements. It stimulated a surge of individualism that splintered opinion into single issues, fragmented political power, and made it more difficult for leaders to lead. For as de Tocqueville observed, "The nearer the people are drawn to the common level of an equal or similar condition, the less prone does each man become to place implicit faith in a certain man or class of men."[19]

Television has helped to alter the fundamental relationship between the people and their government by giving voters instant access to the same information being received by their elected representatives. They now feel they are so well informed about world issues they can form their own opinions in their own homes without any help. For the same reason, congressmen are beguiled into thinking they are wiser than they are. Thanks mainly to television, they also have established what are, in effect, direct individual relationships with their constituents; they no longer are beholden to party bosses or presidents. And all of this has created a major crisis of governance.

### Television and Public Opinion

It has also changed the nature of public opinion and the way opinion functions. Formerly, national opinion was drawn from, and filtered by, an assembly of large political blocs such as party organizations, farmers, big labor, and various sectional interests. Now it is pieced together from an inchoate aggregate of individual views and single-issue positions formed in an atmosphere of militant short-term self-interest rather than concern for a lasting common good. To make matters worse, television arouses emotions like a bugle call, sending public opinion racing ahead of leaders and bypassing the verbal analysis and rational deliberation on which wisdom ultimately depends. "Because TV news accelerates public awareness," says Lloyd Cutler, "the time for response is now even briefer. If an ominous foreign event is featured on TV news, the president and his advisers feel bound to make a response in time for the next evening news broadcast."[20] The result is hasty policy and sometimes disastrous decisions.

Television wields enormous power through its ability to mold this new kind of public opinion. The historian Richard Wade is convinced Japan would have surrendered much sooner if the atom bomb test at Alamogordo in 1945 had been televised for the Japanese people.[21] Scenes of Bull Connor and his swinging cattle prods produced the public pressure which finally launched John Kennedy toward civil rights reforms. Bra-burning demonstrations publicized the women's movement. Television fanned the protests that hurried America's withdrawal from Vietnam and compelled Lyndon Johnson's retirement. The Iranian hostage coverage which Jimmy Carter originally sought later helped defeat him in the 1980 election. Television instantly popularized the invasion of Grenada, making a laughing stock, incidentally, out of carping television pundits who completely misjudged the public mood. As Jody Powell chortled later, "It was sometimes difficult to tell which the American people enjoyed more, seeing the president kick hell out of the Cubans or the press."[22]

Similar emotional signals, multiplied, dramatized, and magnified by television, are manipulating governments in other nations as well. Egyptian President Mubarak was shaken politically by the scenes of failure following the shoot-out in

Malta between his commandos and Palestinian terrorists. The government of Italian Prime Minister Bettino Craxi fell in the aftermath of the *Achille Lauro* affair. And the never-ending scenes of terror and death on Israeli television have powerfully affected that nation's moods and policies.

During a visit in 1985, my wife and I accompanied a friend to an encampment on a barren hill near Jericho to see his son who was serving in a tank unit. Later that night at the hotel, we saw a soldier's funeral procession on television, and suddenly I thought of the young man we had just seen and of how the procession might be for him some day. I thought of how many times that scene must be repeated and how many families must be touched personally. No wonder the Israeli public recoiled against the waste of life in Lebanon, "The Longest War," as Jacobo Timerman called it in a bitter critique that reawakened American memories of Vietnam.

Political pressures, generated by the televised appeals of prisoners' families, were so great that in May 1985, Israel's coalition government released 1,150 Arab prisoners—including Palestinian terrorists—in exchange for three captive Israeli soldiers. Israel had done this before, for example in 1983, when it freed 4,500 captured Palestinian and Lebanese guerrillas for six soldiers held by the PLO. But the smaller exchange in 1985 occurred while Israel was still holding 766 Shiite prisoners. And authorities said this coincidence was one of the circumstances that led to the TWA hijacking that followed.

### U.S. Folly in Lebanon

Confused and fumbling policies have been chiefly responsible for America's own troubled history in Lebanon. But television has been a midwife in nearly everything that has happened. During Israel's 1982 invasion, the public was shocked by gruesome tapes taken after the refugee camp massacres. The White House was horrified and, almost at once, Reagan rushed the marines back into Beirut, apparently against the advice of his defense secretary and the joint chiefs of staff. Among others, Lloyd Cutler argues that if the "public horror would not have been as instantaneous or acute" as television made it, "the response could have been deliberately and perhaps more wisely chosen."[23] As it was, the marines were committed hastily and then later put in the position of taking sides in the Christian-Muslim conflict. This was followed in 1983 by the suicide bombing of the marine bar-racks. Television covered this in awesome detail, rage once more swept through the American public, and the demands that the United States get out of Lebanon became irresistible. The beleaguered marines were pulled out for the second and no doubt last time.

In this case, American feelings, set in motion by events but greatly intensified by television, marched the marines in opposite directions. During the TWA crisis, television affected the govern-ment's tactics in different ways, sometimes helpful, sometimes hurtful, but drove policy in only one direction—toward release of the hostages. The administration was committed never to make any concessions to terrorists, even if hostages were killed, follow-ing the lesson of Munich that appeasement costs more lives than it saves. In numerous television interviews, Kissinger and others warned against any softness. But the public pressures generated by television were even more formidable. At the White House, rescue of the hostages became a higher priority than fixed policy; the release of Israel's prisoners came to appear reasonable; it was clear the United States, without appearing to, would have to find a negotiated solution.

Oakley, the State Department's expert on counter-terrorism, had lived in Beirut fifteen years earlier during an Israeli counter-offensive against guerrilla camps in Lebanon. As the bombs were falling, he recalls looking at the children and thinking how they would become the terrorists of the future, "and that's the way it's turned out." Although there are many reasons for terrorism, he believes media coverage generally increases the incidence by feeding the terrorist's passion for publicity and by promoting the copycat effect. "In the TWA case," he said, "the television coverage initially did increase the pressure on the government to make concessions. This complicated our life immensely. Our other principal concerns were leaks of plans and movements and the problems we faced with the hostage families." He said the government was particularly upset by the Delta Force reports, which officials believe spooked the terrorists into leaving Algiers. "But the coverage was a two-edged sword that cut both ways," he said. "Once Berri and Amal accepted responsibility for the hijacking, the media may have been a help. They put Berri on the hook. He was then identified with the hostages and, in a way, he was stuck."[24] In other words, with the television cameras trained on him, the Amal leader was in the same position as the administration: under pressure to resolve the crisis without harm to the hostages.

So there were more curious twists in a curious story. Television was blamed for risking lives when it reported the Delta Force movements but then credited with helping save lives when it put Berri in the spotlight, because terrorists prefer privacy when they kill. Television initially heightened public fears with its suspenseful, dramatized coverage, but later dissipated those fears with pictures showing that the hostages were in no immediate danger, allowing the government more time to grope toward a solution. Television broke a dozen journalistic laws when it became a participant in the crisis and supplied its own celebrity negotiators, yet it also was a help. It set up the communications, then connected all the parties to each other in such a disguised way that no one had to talk publicly to any one else. It relayed positions back and forth until everyone understood the settlement terms.

Richard C. Holbrooke, a former assistant secretary of state, takes issue with Kissinger's assessment of media damage. "I thought that the TWA coverage was completely weird," he says. "But it reduced the pressure on Reagan to act. It showed the hostages in good health, eating al fresco yet, and in no way in danger. Tasteless, yes, but not damaging to our national interest."[25] Jody Powell and Hodding Carter, of Iranian hostage fame, say the media excesses, bad as they were, did not prolong the crisis or make it more difficult to resolve. While criticizing "mindless moments" and "excesses in taste," a *Washington Post* editorial concluded that television had neither extended the ordeal nor raised the price of the hostages' freedom. "The coverage probably did more damage to journalists than to anybody else," said Powell.[26]

All this is true, but so are several other facts: the hijacking succeeded. One American was killed and forty others were held by terrorists for seventeen days. Public pressures made hostage safety the government's highest priority. Behind the fig leaves of unyielding public stances, negotiations—the "kabuki dance"—went forward. Syria, the Amal's chief backer, was brought in as a secret broker. The demands of the kidnappers were met. The 766 Shiite prisoners were set free, and although this had been planned earlier, it now looked like an Israeli retreat. Berri's prestige was enhanced. Syrian president Haffez Assad was "one of the clear winners," as Livingstone and Terrell E. Arnold concluded.[27]

Washington expressed its gratitude, and in a major speech on July 8, 1985, Reagan conspicuously dropped Syria from his rogue's gallery of terrorist states. The United States did not retaliate as it had threatened. Terrorism against Americans continued, even escalated; military action only came much later in another country, against Gaddafi. And beneath the surface somewhere, there were other unseen marks left on the minds of people in Lebanon, Israel, and other countries in the Middle East, as well as in the United States: New Arab resentments, perhaps, that would one day become another outrage and another crisis; possibly a hardening of American resolve that would lead in a few months to the bombing attacks against Libya, with all that this might portend. Who could be sure?

## No Longer Journalism

What is certain is that the networks will be listed in the final ledger of consequences because they must share responsibility for what occurred. They were not just watchers, standing and observing, but card-carrying participants who helped to shape and direct the unfolding drama. They merged with the crisis, became part of it, and action and coverage became so intertwined it was hard to tell one from the other. Reporters were no longer just reporters, journalism no longer just journalism but a unique bonding of newsmaking and news reporting, dictated by television's special nature and lying beyond traditional definitions of news. This is the central issue that arose with particular force during the TWA case. In the long term, it is more important than immediate effects in a specific crisis because it strikes at television's identity. When a network anchor is making news, he is neither a government official nor a journalist; he is a hybrid. He has no credentials in the first role and loses them in the second.

The problem is not entirely unique. Mingling with great men and great events is an exhilarating experience that has always tempted journalists to try their own hand at making policy. Winston Churchill, who included journalism in his collection of careers, once said that he expected history to be kind to him because he intended to write it. From William Randolph Hearst to Walter Lippmann, a long line of newspaper publishers, editors, columnists, and reporters has been involved in shaping national policy. I remember when Peter Lisagor of the Chicago *Daily News* and I had a lengthy private session with John F. Kennedy. We expected to beat the town with a headline exclusive. But when we checked our memories on what we had learned—at the time, you didn't take notes or tape presidential interviews—we were startled. We didn't have any story because we had spent the whole time telling Kennedy how he should be running the country. Even more humiliating, he didn't follow our advice.

There are instances where newspapermen have manipulated events, as well as offered advice, to affect national decisions. Hearst did it with headlines like "How Do You Like the Journal's War?" which ran when the explosion of the Battleship Maine in 1898 virtually guaranteed he would get the war he had been promoting. Lippmann did it with analysis, not only in his columns but even more effectively in an endless stream of personal letters and private conversations with world leaders. He used to sit quietly with ordinary reporters at presidential press conferences but then disappear into the salons of power. As much as any anchorman today, in some respects more than any anchorman, he influenced leaders, policy, and events. Moreover, he did much of this privately. When the German peace treaty was being negotiated, he wrote urgently to John Foster Dulles, an American delegate, warning against "a separate peace" that would exclude Russia. For a variety of reasons, he explained later, he could not discuss his argument in a column because of the impact it would have on the negotiating process.[28]

Lippmann's policymaking violated the canon of ethics that says journalists should stand apart from the public business they cover. What is more relevant to the present discussion is the difference between Lippmann's power and the kind now exercised by television's stars. Lippmann moved in the corridors of the Eastern Establishment, among the chosen in Georgetown and along Massachusetts and Pennsylvania avenues, where the great issues were debated and decided away from the masses. His column in the New York *Herald-Tribune* was syndicated to other newspapers, but it was more a showcase for statesmen than a mover of public opinion. His real power came from his remarkable ability to influence the elite in those simpler years when the elite still ruled Washington.

All this was changed in the new world of mass democracy and mass communications. Noisy, jostling television reporters and media-eager politicians pushed into the private club rooms of George Kennan and James Reston. The Eastern Establishment fell on hard times and the elites, like Miniver Cheevy, "sighed for what was not." Thanks mainly to television, their power was dispersed outward, and the general public intruded more and more into the daily affairs of the country, mass participatory democracy in action. With instant information and instant reactions, public opinion now tends to operate directly on policy, especially in crises when emotions run high. And it can command; that is the difference. Lippmann could only persuade leaders; he could not coerce. But television, with its special ability to mobilize and transmit opinion, can compel action. To a degree columnists and newspapers cannot match, it is also able to create and change the events on which opinion is based. News is custom-made to its specifications by presidents and terrorists, by Michael Deavers and David Garths, so that its influence is circular and self-reinforcing.

Television's power is unique, therefore, and so are the consequences of what it does. When it mixes reporting with newsmaking, entertainment, and celebrity promotion, it is revising the way people receive their news. It is altering their perception of problems and how they reach conclusions. Together with computers, in fact, it is changing the nature of public knowledge itself. All of this is happening, moreover, in the presence of rapidly advancing technology and institutional ferment. The coverage excesses in the TWA case cannot be fully understood, for example, without a sense of the role changes being forced on the networks by increasingly aggressive local news operations. As a result, television's relationship to society is still in transition and its news culture still evolving. It has left the age of print and the traditions of newspapers, but it has not yet arrived at its own destination. It is still finding its way toward traditions that will fit its special character.

This is the opportunity and the challenge. Opportunity because television news practices have been changing rapidly and are open to more change. Challenge because there are inherent conflicts between television's impressionistic nature and its responsibilities to a society in need of a trustworthy journalism. Nowhere is this more evident than in the coverage of terrorism.

# 5 / A Better Way

Anyone who raises problems is expected to have solutions. That is the American way. The saliva test for a congressman is to present him with a crisis. If he immediately introduces a bill and announces the crisis is over, you know he is a congressman. As the federal deficit approached catastrophe, the answer was simple: the Gramm-Rudman-Hollings Bill. The problem, if not the deficit, disappeared forthwith. America's faith in its ability to climb any mountain was born on the frontier, nurtured by success, and soliloquized by John Kennedy, so it is very strong. It is also wrong. What is true elsewhere in the world is true also in the United States. There are no solutions for unsolvable problems and recognition of this fact is the beginning of wisdom.

The United States has learned, at considerable expense, that for all its great power it cannot control events even in small nations. That was the lesson of Vietnam and it is now the lesson of Nicaragua and Lebanon. The only choice in the terrible confusion of Lebanon is to leave it on the stove, cooking in the juices of its own history. And if there is ever to be an answer to international terrorism, it will be found somewhere over the horizon when the forces reorganizing the post-colonial world have run their course. For the present, only containment through suppressive counter-measures seems possible.

The dilemmas of television news need to be approached in this same spirit of limited possibility because the most serious problems are also the most intractable. They emerge from a conflict of natures which cannot be repealed—the nature of television, the nature of governments, the nature of terrorism. American television is what it is. It can no more change itself into a newspaper or an academic journal than a politician can avoid a microphone. It is headlines, pictures, personalities, entertainment, and emotions, acting and interacting in a free and competitive environment. No matter how they are apportioned, these elements remain; they may be helpful to terrorists and hurtful to governments, but they are a given. Even so, there are many things television can do, short of changing its nature, to make itself less useful to bombers and hijackers. And it would be acting in its own self-interest as well as society's because its own legitimacy is at risk.

As mentioned earlier, television newscasters justify everything they do by the people's "need to know" and claim all the press freedoms guaranteed by the Constitution. But there is no compelling need for celebrity journalism, entertainment, or emotional hype. These cannot be disguised as news and passed off as a national resource that must forever stand free of interference by president or Congress. Making false claims under the First Amendment is to invite the very government intervention it was intended to prevent. Jody Powell cut to the heart of the issue when he said that "tasteless, exploitative, sensationalized coverage undermines public support for the legal protections that allow journalists to do their job. An obsession with tonight's ratings to the detriment of such fundamental long-term interests is not only irresponsible, it's just plain stupid."[1]

Another point of vulnerability is television's role as a newsmaker and news participant. It is now too deeply enmeshed in government and the world's business, and too influential, to pretend it is just a eunuch in the throne room, only an observer and critic. It has to assume responsibilities commensurate with its power. When newscasters create, shape, and change events, they must accept the blame for what happens as well the applause. Despite the misgivings of ABC's Ted Koppel and others, they need to consider the social and political consequences of what they do. They have to subordinate competition and sensation to higher public priorities. In short, they must impose restraints on their own behavior or risk the unwelcome alternative of government restrictions.

Institutions, of course, are extremely resistant to self-correction; the legal profession, for instance, clings stubbornly to its processes even while they are strangling justice. Reforms therefore need to be imposed by outside forces and inspired by such base sentiments as personal benefit and institutional self-interest. Doctors opposed third-party payment until the public demanded it, and they saw their incomes improve. Similarly, newspapermen, the original mold from which arrogance was made, usually yield only to public pressures. After Watergate, reporters were so overwhelmed by their importance they rushed into a whole range of excesses from official-bashing to advocacy journalism. Criticism rose, libel suits proliferated, and newspaper readership fell. Sensing trouble, the profession finally discovered a crisis of public credibility and started making repairs. With television, as with newspapers, public criticism and self-interest are the most effective instruments of reform. Only if these are brought forcefully to bear will television news be motivated to subordinate ratings to the larger public good in its coverage of terrorism.

### The Show's the Thing

The most obvious starting point for reform is the feature that chiefly sets television apart from journalism and accounts for most of its difficulties in the coverage of terrorism. This is the fact that it is first and foremost an entertainment medium. In theory, if not always in practice, journalism is supposed to be concerned with actuality. To be sure, most newspapers try to enliven their pages with features, pictures, comic strips, games, and miscellaneous other forms of static entertainment. They usually do not succeed, which explains the drabness of many newspapers, but even if they did, the result would be only peripheral to the main business—news. The situation in television is exactly the reverse: entertainment is the main business and news is the sideline. And even the news, because of television's nature, has to be cast in an entertainment form complete with stages, stars, and moving pictures.

More than anything else, entertainment is the magnet that constantly draws television news away from factual reporting and from its mission simply to inform. There is nothing inherently wrong about presenting news in an entertaining way. No one expects television to be as colorless as the *Wall Street Journal*. But all those happy talk shows that were in vogue a few years ago were a travesty of the news. And while many of the entertainment techniques now being used work well for some stories, they are inappropriate for others. They almost always misfire in the case of terrorism where the issues are grim and emotions run high. The entertainment factor needs to be modified, then, and television news practices moved closer to hard news in order to avoid the exploitative excesses that marked the TWA coverage. A number of related issues come to mind.

## Theatrical Devices

The repeated replaying of dramatic tapes of terrorists and hostages is almost always done for impact rather than informing audiences. Those brief vignettes of people under stress interspersed throughout the CBS morning news coverage had only one purpose: to hype viewer emotions. In terrorism cases especially, these artificial stimulants can overheat a crisis and create pressures that unduly influence government responses. Theatrical devices that manipulate factual material only for dramatic effect should not be used. As Krauthammer observed in *Time,*

> . . . . If much of the coverage is indeed not news but entertainment—bizarre guerrilla theater that outdoes "Network"—then television might quite properly place voluntary limits on it, as it does on . . . explicit sex. Why not on explicit terror? There is no reason why all the news of a terrorist event, like news of a rape, cannot be transmitted in some form. But in the interest of decency, diplomacy and our own self-respect, it need not be live melodrama.[2]

## Pictures

Cameramen often focus closely on an isolated scene, a single face or child, to create and heighten drama so that a small disturbance, for example, looks like a riot when it finally appears on the screen. Pictures like this libel reality, create false viewer reactions, and promote rather than lessen tensions. They should be avoided. Pictures that show terrorist smiles but not the blood they spill—children wounded by American bombs in Tripoli but not the victims of Gaddafi's atrocities—need somehow to be put into better context despite the obvious difficulties.

## Celebrities

Anchormen and star correspondents are here to stay; personalities are the life of television. Whatever Sam Donaldson's talents are as a reporter, they do not matter much; it is his saturnine face and word-biting manner that sells. When the "big feet" wade into a news story they often create so many waves they change the event itself. David Hartman's morning chat with Berri and the Conwells was enterprising television but it changed the whole tone of the TWA crisis. And "when network anchormen go on TV every hour," as Kissinger says, "it creates a crisis atmosphere."

Thanks to satellites, the anchormen can roam the world without ever leaving their stage sets in New York, conferring with statesmen and pulling their stories together while viewers watch and mere beat reporters serve as props. In an effort to provide something their local television competitors cannot match, the anchors have also been taking their shows on the road lately, which explains why they were scattered from Texas to Moscow in 1986 when the big story of Ferdinand Marcos's fall from power broke in the Philippines thousands of miles away.

Coverage of foreign affairs by both newspapers and television is already being damaged by a trend toward "parachute" journalism in which reporters no longer are stationed in many countries but only drop in when there is a breaking story. The situation is made worse when celebrity journalism adds its own distorting effects. The effects can also be dangerous in the case of terrorism, where the stakes are high and the dilemmas great for both journalism and government.

Television should lower its celebrity profile to the lowest feasible level in terrorist stories by emphasizing straight factual reporting by correspondents in the field and eliminating posturing interventions and long-distance interviewing by network anchors. This would move the coverage closer to hard news, modulate the emotional pitch of news shows, and help curb the compulsion of television stars to intrude into the president's role of crisis management.

### Staging

Manufacturing news and staging events especially for television are so routine now that almost no one thinks about it any more. During the last presidential election campaign, platoons of media manipulators worked full-time for their candidates. Reagan's men even tried to bar reporters from airport crowds so that his handshaking could be taped but his impromptu comments censored. The substance has been hollowed out of political conventions so that nothing is left except a Hollywood shell. All of this came as a surprise to Lloyd Cutler when he worked in the White House, and he offered a blunt commentary in *Foreign Policy*. "Print and TV journalists ought to expose the tacit conspiracy of silence about staging," he wrote, "whether practiced by revered network announcers or by politicians in and out of office. Staging is making people or events appear different from what they really are. Staging of course has its place in the creative arts, but in the arts its use is not concealed from the audience. The staging of TV news, political press conferences, and public addresses is concealed from the audience. Not to mince words, it is a fraud."[3]

Richard Wald at ABC concedes that "staging is a terrific problem and I don't know the answer. But I don't accept the idea that terrorism would go away if there weren't any." He cites Northern Ireland as a place where terrorism continues with relatively little news coverage.[4] In Beirut, however, staging was a major terrorist activity, and it created serious coverage problems. One was the cumulative effect of all the interviews and press conferences. These may have had a specific news value when considered individually and at a single time. But when they grew in number and the tapes were then played over and over again, what began as news was converted into a media spectacle. A second problem was that it was very difficult to clue viewers to the real nature of what they were seeing on their screens, a hostage saying one thing, for example, but almost certainly thinking something else.

While staging may be as incurable as the common cold, as Wald suggests, the morbid sequelae can be modified in at least three ways. First, in terrorist cases staged interviews and press conferences should never be broadcast live or in the form of raw footage. Only the hard news, carefully edited and fully explained, should be carried. Second, these events should only be reported when they are new to audiences and not repeated night and day for theatrical and promotional reasons. And, finally, newscasters need to use more visually effective methods to balance pictures with disclaimers so that viewers are adequately alerted to any misleading news content. Words alone cannot compete with dramatic tapes.

### Promoting Terrorists

Even if television were stripped of all of its entertainment techniques, the terrorists would still be standing there in Beirut or Algiers or someplace else in the center of the story—in the center of American fears and anger. Television would still be the chief liaison for everyone involved. Public frustrations with the villains would fall also on their messengers for it is infuriating to see kidnappers and murderers given a world stage to intimidate the United States and broadcast their propaganda. It was this, more than anything else, that brought the critics out in force during the TWA crisis. And it framed what is probably the most difficult coverage issue in these cases: whether, how, and to what extent terrorists should be publicized.

### News Blackout?

Britain's Prime Minister Margaret Thatcher, who was nearly killed by an IRA bomb, spoke for many critics when she called in effect for a news blackout. She said the media should agree never to report or show "anything which could assist the terrorists' morale or their cause."[5] Kissinger, in a television interview during the TWA ordeal, said, "I think what the media ought to consider is not to carry anything including the terrorists. If the terrorists didn't see in this a means of getting their message across, there would be less dog and pony shows like this."[6] Most journalists argue, however, that cutting off coverage would only feed rumors, increase fears, and incite terrorists to ever-greater atrocities. John Chancellor says, "People need to see terrorism. The alternative is to close down society, which is what the Red Brigades wanted to do in Italy."[7]

Amid these differing views is a fundamental issue: the right of the American people to know what others know. When terrorists go public, so to speak, that becomes a fact that is immediately available to those present, at a press conference in Beirut or wherever. They are seen and heard and, whether government officials like it or not, the word spreads through a thousand channels. Pictures of Nabih Berri appear on television screens in Lebanon and scores of other countries. The arrival of the TWA hostages in Damascus is broadcast throughout Syria as well as in the United States. The scenes of devastation at the Rome and Vienna airports and later in the West Berlin discotheque are carried everywhere.

Staging and news manipulation are troublesome factors in the coverage of terrorists. But to blot out the actual event is too drastic a cure. Even wartime censorship did not cut Americans completely off from enemy scenes or propaganda during World War II. No one bothered to prevent GIs from listening to Tokyo Rose. The networks were free to use tapes of Ho Chi Minh during the Vietnam War. A news blackout denies Americans what others know. It moves news coverage more deeply into news management. In the long run, this could add to the problems of fact and illusion that already exist and undermine public trust in the source of information on which national decisions are made. Columbia University's J. Bowyer Bell, an authority on terrorism, summed up the dilemma in his *A Time of Terror*:

> Of all the foundations of free democratic society, that most basic— the freedom to know, to be informed—has guaranteed that such knowledge and such information can be fashioned by the fanatic through the conduit of the media eye. To close that eye would erode a fundamental right, would close an open society. Yet not to do so assures future massacres.[8]

A total news blackout also is not feasible. Thanks to our ethnocentric perspective, the whole debate is centered on the American networks; the idea seems to be that if they would just switch off their cameras, terrorists would never get their pictures taken. The fact is that the networks do not even control the local stations in this country, much less the rest of the world. Torrents of news now flood the earth; thanks to technology, national borders are breaking down so that more and more news is penetrating even into closed societies like Russia. It seemed only minutes after U.S. bombers attacked Libya that street demonstrations broke out in dozens of capitals all through Europe, the Middle East, and in even more distant nations. The emotions of millions of people were aroused almost instantly by a communications system that no one controls.

Foreign news organizations are active nearly everywhere, sometimes putting more correspondents and cameramen into the field than the U.S. networks. Any reporter who has covered a story the Japanese are pursuing will confirm that. "In Iran," Chancellor recalls, "the pictures and the coverage would have gone all over the world if only one camera crew had been allowed in from Botswana TV. . . . Controlling one nation's journalists does not mean controlling all journalism. Yet much of our thinking is based on national and not international concepts. National sovereignty is one thing; journalistic sovereignty, in a free society, is much harder to accomplish."[9]

### Terrorist Interviews

While total blackouts are impractical, reportorial moderation is both possible and needed. Terrorist news can be reported without giving hijackers and their spokesmen a free ride on television; indeed, their Helsinki rights would not be destroyed if they were given no air time at all. In general, therefore, terrorist interviews like NBC's rendezvous with Mohammad Abbas should not be aired. As David Broder of the *Washington Post* argued in a powerful syllogism:

> 1. Terrorism is "a form of warfare . . . not random violence against individuals" and it is "waged by enemies of the United States . . ."
> 2. "Terrorism, like all other forms of warfare, is intended for political or geopolitical ends. . . ."
> 3. "The real goal of terrorism is political" and in democracies like the United States, this means influencing public opinion. For this reason, "the ultimate objective of terrorists is to capture not individual hostages but the instruments of public opinion of which television is by far the most powerful."
> 4. "Therefore, from those premises, I conclude that the essential ingredient of any effective anti-terrorist policy must be the denial to the terrorists of access to mass media outlets." It is a "crucial question" whether this is best accomplished by media self-restraint or government control. "But whatever the means that are chosen, I think the end has to be the denial of access to those terrorists."[10]

Roone Arledge insists this is ABC's policy; he explained that Berri was aired only because he was considered a moderate intermediary rather than a practicing terrorist. In the TWA postmortems, other network news executives said they, too, were opposed to giving gunmen airtime, but did not rule out this possibility in some future case. For NBC, the possibility emerged the minute it felt the lure of an exclusive interview with Abbas. Its news values were then subordinated to the competitive lust to establish an edge over CBS in the ratings war among the evening news shows.

Newscasters can keep American audiences fully informed in terrorist cases without surrendering their cameras. For example, if a producer needs a picture to establish a hijacker's identity, he can give it the silent screen treatment while a correspondent delivers the news voice-over. The hijacker himself does not have to be put on the air expounding his own views. Moreover, the segment should only be carried on a spot news basis; tapes should not be repeated on every network time cycle and again on hundreds of local news shows until 30- or 60-second bites become a groundswell of propaganda. Terrorists or their mouthpieces should not be aired just because a producer is trying to keep his story running or needs pictures, or because the film can be ballyhooed as an exclusive. Practices and devices that are harmless in harmless stories can be dangerous in dangerous stories.

All tapes should be carefully edited before they are aired. Live coverage or raw tapes should never be broadcast because doing so converts journalism into a recording machine and—in hostage crises—can do all sorts of harm or even endanger lives. In his terrorism memo to his troops, NBC's Grossman said this procedure was "preferable" but that there could be "urgent circumstances" in which interviews might be aired live, in which case correspondents should duly counsel the audience.[11] This is the immediacy problem discussed before: television's compulsion to jump on the tube with any new bulletin or development, not because the public has to have the information immediately but to beat the other networks. This cannot be defended in terrorism cases; there are no valid excuses for live or raw coverage; on the contrary, there is an overriding public need to proceed with great deliberation rather than frenetic haste.

### Propaganda Control

Even if terrorists are covered, many critics say the networks should agree not to photograph them making their demands while they are holding hostages. "I don't object to the simple setting of demands," says Kissinger. "I object to letting the terrorists tape performances for American television during which they state their demands. That may create an incentive to kidnap people in order to get on television. . . ."[12] It is too easy to dismiss his point with television's glib statement that American audiences are not taken in by the propaganda. They are affected even if they are not taken in and, as we have seen, challenging the United States on television does a great deal to promote terrorists among their own followers, with other terrorists, and with wider constituencies.

ABC's Jennings says Kissinger's proposal would be "worth considering" but that the way the system now works the terrorists have become "a legitimate part of the news story."[13] Yes, but the terrorists do not have to tell the story themselves. Reporters can do it for them; that is what they are paid for. When terrorist demands are first made, they obviously are news; they need to be reported, with disclaimers, but without the usual dramatizations and needless repetition. And they should be surrounded by a great deal more explanation and context than was the case in Beirut. Terrorists' statements need to be balanced by other facts but not drowned in commentary by experts, officials, and assorted anchors. This only hyperventilates the story and unduly raises public emotions. Calm, factual reporting presented in a standard news format, with meaning and background, is the best way to convert exploitation into journalism.

### Terrorist Tapes

During the Flight 847 hijacking, as we have seen, all three networks aired a videotaped interview with the hostages which the Amal had conducted and apparently edited to eliminate any negative publicity. The official justification was that it proved the hostages were alive and, with a wide margin for error, indicated their condition. An unofficial reason was that it was good television in a highly competitive situation. Now, it appears, all the networks agree that homemade terrorist tapes should never be used except in extreme emergencies, and then only if they are heavily surrounded by audience warnings. What these emergencies might be is unclear, but there is a more satisfactory solution than broadcasting doctored tapes. This would be simply to report the tapes' existence, describe what they might indicate, and discuss their dubious origin, but not actually air them.

This problem is more ominous than it seems at first glance; the reason is onrushing technology. Home video cameras, videotape recorders, and other state-of-the-art equipment are becoming as common as guns, and as affordable. Until recently, terrorists have been forced to depend on the networks and other large organizations to do their television work for them because they did not have the expensive equipment or knowhow. Now they are getting both, and other sophisticated equipment like portable ground stations is on the way. Terrorists will be able to manufacture and tape their own terror campaigns. W. D. Livingstone, a senatorial aide specializing in terrorism, says, "Such a development forebodes a new era in terrorism and is likely to kindle serious problems for the media and government officials."[14]

In January 1985, he noted, terrorists produced a fifty-six-second videotape of an American hostage making a plea for government help. Visnews, a television news service, made the tape available to NBC which aired an excerpt. A few months later, a Shiite Muslim girl, only seventeen years old, was taped explaining why she was willing to sacrifice her life and urging other girls to join in the National Resistance Front against Israeli troops in Lebanon. She then drove a Peugeot with 400 pounds of explosives into an Israeli convoy, killing two soldiers. In April 1986, a pro-Libyan group said it had hanged a British hostage because of Margaret Thatcher's cooperation in the U.S. air raid on Libya and as proof delivered a videotape of a man hanging from a scaffold. The next horror that authorities now anticipate is that terrorists will begin making videotapes of actual attacks, showing the bombings, all the action which the network cameras miss. "Just as public relations firms now assist the media when they cover news events," said Livingstone, "the threat exists that terrorists will begin to assist reporters. . . by recording on film or videotape their bombings or hostage incidents to strengthen the impact."[15]

## Television Diplomacy

During the TWA ordeal, Roger Mudd of NBC was only trying to be helpful, no doubt, when he made the suggestion: "Why does not the Israeli government, why does not the United States government, go ahead and swallow its pride just for a few days to facilitate this [hostage-Shiite] release?" Unfortunately, his effort was not appreciated because there is a widely held view that the government should do the negotiating in hostage situations.

Network executives say they share this opinion. "Any reporter who takes on the role of negotiator or middleman, as has happened in prison riots and hostage situations," said Grossman of NBC, "forfeits his role as a reporter. When he becomes a player, he is no longer an observer. Television's role is to cover what is happening and not try to change the event or influence the participants."[16] The problem is not the goal: it is the practice. In the very act of running back and forth between terrorists and government officials, reporters tend to become involved in the story. To Berri, "What are your demands?"; to the White House, "Are you asking Israel to free the Shiite prisoners?"; to everybody else, "Do you think Reagan's doing the right thing?" A lot of stan-

dard journalistic practices drive reporters over the fine line between observation and participation.

To reduce the danger of participation, reporters need to begin
by suspending some of their normal habits. Get the terrorist
demands and the government's position, to be sure, but cut back
on the usual amphetamines—the roundup of conflicting views
and weighty commentaries. These are seldom of historic significance, but they create a lot of hoopla and often have the effect
of moving the policy debate out of Washington and into television studios. Newscasters also need to be sensitive to the special
problems involved in hostage crises and change their reporting
style to fit. This would mean framing questions very carefully
so that they elicit facts but do not lead reporter and subject into
the middle of the negotiating process.

Television anchors are a special problem. Their high visibility
and perceived power mean they cannot ring up terrorist leaders
in Beirut and secretaries of state in Washington, while millions
of viewers are kibitzing, and pass it all off as just old-fashioned
reporting. This automatically affects the process. "Anchormen
thousands of miles from the scene of terrorism and with only
a slivered, incomplete view of what is happening," says Fred
Friendly, "should not attempt to interview the terrorist. It is not
only star promotion; it elevates hostage takers or keepers to the
status of heads of states."[17] There are many other less sensitive
occasions when the stars can do their reporting calisthenics and
attract promotion; in hostage situations, legmen should do the
field interviews. This would help to minimize television's unap-
preciated intrusion into government and reduce the incidence
of those self-serving statements:

RATHER: "Berri told me that if Israel agrees. . . ."

### Hostages and Families

Hostages and the families of hostages are the most emotional
of all the issues in the journalism of terror. They are the stand-
ins for our own terror, our own fears, all that is bound up in
life and death. "Man has created death," said Yeats, and television creates its image. Like all great drama, it makes strangers
our friends and neighbors and their experiences our experiences.
It multiplies emotions many times over and intensifies already
existing attitudes, personal and political. When the behavior of
hostages conflicts with preconceived ideas, differences are

sharpened. When reactions are magnified by media exploitation, they confuse and complicate crisis management. "In hostage situations, when millions get to see and, to some extent, know individual victims," says Grossman, "the pressure to free the captives intensifies. The more the people know, the more the authorities feel impelled to act if only to overcome the appearance of impotence."[18] All of this calls for sensitivity, restraint, and special journalistic handling. Several issues are involved.

### Hostage Interviews

Many critics insist that interviews with hostages should not be aired at all because they are captives speaking under duress and because it helps terrorists, humiliates America, and puts undue pressure on the government to compromise. "The networks wouldn't show a picture of an actual rape on television," said Kissinger. "There are some decencies that you must observe."[19] On the other hand, there are strong countervailing arguments: the hostages' own need for friendly contact, the legitimate desire of relatives and other Americans to know their condition, and the fact that public exposure tends to protect their lives. As *Time's* Thomas Griffith put it, "The belief that every American life is of value can indeed be exploited by others, but it is part of what makes us the kind of people we are."[20]

All things considered, the condition of the hostages is news that should be covered. Although still pictures and newspaper reporting might accomplish the same purpose, as they did in years gone by, television is now the medium of choice; television interviews can deliver the essential news, but they must be carefully edited, restrained, and given only limited air time so that they do not exploit the hostages or unduly exacerbate the crisis. Sensitive, responsible handling is critical to avoid the sensationalism which marred the TWA coverage.

### Propaganda Pawns

Everyone has a standard image of how prisoners should behave in captivity. So when the TWA hostages were delivered to press conferences and restaurant interviews in Beirut, it was assumed that they were afraid for their lives. The guards and guns were an obvious restraint on candor and supposedly, therefore, the captives did not really mean what they were saying. Obviously, they could not possibly have been treated very well nor could they have had any real sympathy or understanding for the Amal cause. So critics raised a hue and cry with the networks because the hostages were being exploited, used to establish a moral equivalence between their own kidnapping and Israel's seizure of 766 Shiites. They said that even if hostages are put on the air to prove they are alive, they should not be allowed to air propaganda. But the argument was laced with emotional overtones and complexities because hostage behavior did not conform to pre-established mind-sets.

When he interviewed three of the hostages in a restaurant, ABC's Charles Glass explained that if the interview "might jeopardize their security or be used for Amal propaganda, we would not do it. I whispered that all they had to do was blink, and I would tell Amal that our camera was not working and we would all leave." When the guards left the group alone several times, he said, "the three Americans did not change their statements or behavior, on or off camera."[21] It turned out that the hostages' spokesman, Allyn Conwell, was very knowledgeable about the Middle East and genuinely believed the Amal had a legitimate complaint. Several other hostages seemed to be similarly disposed, even after they were released. In other words, actual hostage attitudes can conflict with emotionally charged presumptions, which raises at least two basic questions.

One is whether producers and editors should take it on themselves to censor speech because they believe the speech is not free. Another is whether they should suppress hostage statements simply because they promote a position or cause Americans do not like. In both cases, the answer of experience is no; hostage crises are not the same as rape. Hostage interviews are humiliating and complicate policy. But tinkering with what the public can see and hear is a greater hazard when unknown facts and uncertain assumptions are linked to subjective news judgments.

What is equally true, however, is that liberty is not license. As argued earlier, journalists need to consider consequences and take responsibility when they are manipulating events for their own purposes. To deny the public essential facts because of subjective concerns is one thing; it is something else to distort those facts by presenting them out of context in a hyped and misleading way. It is irresponsible to put the hostages on live or to run raw footage of interviews, the way CNN did in one case. All tapes should be seen ahead of time, edited, and put into perspective.

It is imperative to explain the circumstances of the interview, the assumption that the hostages are talking under duress, the background of any statements they make. "There should be the cardinal rule," says John Chancellor, "that if the tape of the interview with the hostages goes for three minutes, we should break in to warn the people that this came from the terrorists, that the hostages may be under great stress, etc. The key is don't put it on the air or in a newspaper unless it is edited and fully explained. This is not censorship or social engineering. It's journalism."[22]

In addition, television must at all costs avoid exploitation; to use hostages merely to heighten drama and hype news shows is an offense to them, to the public, and to journalism. As in other situations discussed earlier, hostage interviews should be carried only at the time when they are news; they should not be repeated endlessly on every local channel and national network.

### Hostage Families

The one point on which critics and the networks are in accord is that family interviews were so excessive during the TWA crisis that they became a tasteless invasion of privacy and badly unbalanced the entire story. There is pressure now to reduce coverage of families even when they are eager themselves to publicize their cause. ABC's Roone Arledge would eliminate family interviews altogether if he had his way. Many of these, however, originate with local television stations in hostage hometowns where, generally speaking, there is less news experience and fewer outside restraints. The problem, therefore, is far from solved; interviews will continue in some form. But local newscasters, as well as network correspondents, should at least avoid making things worse with recklessly insensitive reporting. Among other things, they should avoid firing loaded political questions at relatives who are in a poor emotional position to make sophisticated judgments, even if they are knowledgeable. Families should not be prodded into taking policy positions that create artificial pressures on government officials and involve both families and reporters in the negotiating process.

## Competition

The driving force in the scramble for interviews with hostages and their families is not the zeal to inform but the zeal to outdo the opposition. Most of the TWA excesses—volume, hype, pressure for exclusives, tastelessness—can be traced to an atmosphere of fierce competition. As Friendly put it, "the root of the evils of lost context lies in the haphazard frenzy of ratings and competition and the irresponsible orgy of the mindless drive for exclusives. Those cliches, often shrouded in secrecy, are an echo of the yellow journalism of a different age and have no place in an era of instantaneous communication."[23]

The competitive energies released in a major story become uncontrollable because there are so many players with different goals and standards: television at the local, national, and international level, terrorist leaders and government officials, plus a volatile mix of reality, propaganda, and news manipulation. Also, unfortunately, sensation frequently offers higher rewards than responsibility. During the police bombing fiasco in Philadelphia in 1985, one television station decided as a civic duty to be ultra-restrained in its coverage. "It was a model of responsibility," a network commentator observed privately. "An award-winner, except that their ratings went into the cellar compared to the other stations. This fact was not lost on everyone else in the business."

## Excessive Volume

Intense competition drives television coverage to greater and greater extremes, with every network and station trying to outdo the other until the sheer volume of bulletins and special reports is overwhelming, the sense of crisis is grossly exaggerated, and news becomes an absurd contortion bearing little relationship to reality. Even network executives were appalled by what happened during the TWA crisis. CBS's Howard Stringer said the networks simply had to quit acting like "squabbling monsters" and compete not for exclusives but for accuracy and thoughtfulness. At NBC, Grossman said, "interruptions of the regular schedule must be done with caution and only when there is something new to report. The common sense rule is to provide credible, factual coverage without endangering life or hampering authorities."[24] Displaying the resolution that always follows rather than precedes disaster, and inspired by massive public criticism, all three networks solemnly vowed in the future to cut back on bulletins and program break-ins and in general to keep their coverage volume under some reasonable control.

But good resolutions, even if they were to survive in another big story, are not enough. Major changes in news organization and practices are also required. For one thing, television needs to eliminate the massive duplication between network and local television news operations, at least in terrorist cases. At present, the local stations are moving into national and international news with time slots the networks cannot match. Eager to display their new capabilities, they flood television screens with their own coverage of terrorists, hostages, and hostage families. And this is added to the reports being rushed onto the air by feverishly competitive networks so that the cumulative effect is enormous.

The underlying reason for this is that the networks no longer have the monopoly they once had in non-local news and are groping for a new role that will assure their continuing importance. Otherwise, they could become just a news service like the Associated Press. It is reminiscent of the career change television itself forced on the print media some years ago. For a long time after television's arrival, newspapers kept publishing bulletins, changing headlines every hour, and even putting out extras in the mistaken belief they were still in the breaking news business. It was only belatedly that they awoke to the fact that television had taken over the headline concession and they had been transferred to a more reflective branch of journalism. The sooner the networks and the local news staffs sort out their future relationship, the sooner it may be possible to eliminate some of the overlap that now makes the parts of television coverage loom larger than the whole.

### News Strategy

Another factor that contributes to coverage overkill is the manipulation of news to get the maximum possible mileage out of a major story in terms of attracting and holding audiences. Strategic competitive thinking—which is just as important in the news business as it is in diplomacy, if not as cosmic—is most easily seen in so-called running stories that catch and hold the public's attention for days, weeks, or even longer as in the Iranian hostage case. Every smart producer or newspaper editor, especially one dependent on street sales, starts thinking strategy the minute he wakes up in the morning, even before he yawns. While the beat reporter may be waiting for something to happen, the producer is worrying about the next show and the one after that. He is creating, exploiting, and expanding news all the time to capture more viewers. If a major story already has broken, he is buzzing with ideas on how to get new angles, increase the impact, keep it rolling even if there are no naturally occurring new developments. The idea is to create enough interest to carry audiences along for as many days as possible and build ratings. When a producer senses a lull, he develops an exclusive or an "enterprise feature" to hold interest until the next piece of real news appears. At some moment, he will know intuitively that a running story is beginning to die; then he will begin building a new story in order to maintain maximum audience stimulation, and the whole cycle is repeated. Meanwhile, other producers, not to mention newspaper editors, are going through the same process, each trying to outdo the other with the result that the overall volume of coverage grows exponentially.

At the same time, newsmakers are working on their own strategic agendas. As we have seen, Reagan runs a sophisticated media management program, with specific themes at different times, like economic recovery, tax reform, or Strategic Defense Initiative. In the TWA case, the strategy was to keep a low profile, and consequently there was little White House-generated news. After the air raid on Libya, however, the administration wanted to get its case to the public quickly, so Reagan made a televised speech the same night, and Vice President Bush, the secretaries of state and defense, and assorted other officials hurried onto the talk shows early the next morning. This time there was a great deal of White House news.

All of this, of course, is a form of news manipulation, but there are differences: the White House is supposed to make news; reporters are supposed to cover or uncover news, not make it. In the Flight 847 case, most celebrity interviews and enterprise stories were not natural occurrences but the creations of strategy-minded producers. This kind of make-believe news should be ruled out in future crises. No vital information would be lost to the nation. Both the volume of coverage and the index of public emotions would be mercifully reduced. Hard, factual reporting would replace hype and illusion and provide a more rational basis for wise decision-making by national leaders.

### Promotion

A third example of a competitive practice that contributes to excess in terrorism coverage is promotion. For an entertainment medium like television, promotion is a life force. Anchormen complain about how little time they have on their evening news shows but use gobs of it to plug news items coming up after the commercials, what's being featured later on "Nightline," the top stars who will be interviewed the next morning, and what to look for the following evening. It is surprising there is any time left for news. In the presence of history, the promotion mills run overtime, bragging about exclusives, boosting news specials, and promising more excitement to come: "Just stay tuned or you'll miss something." Most of the plugs are read by the anchors rather than announcers so the hype and the news are served in the same soup. The total effect is to soften the edges of news and create an atmosphere of hustle and illusion. More serious, in terrorist stories, the promos artificially heighten the sense of crisis and distort reality. The horn blowing was so loud in the TWA case that, as Fred Friendly testified at a congressional hearing, even the Super Bowl could not match it. "The Super Bowl is a game," he said. "We can't go on treating terrorism, which is a form of war, as if it were a game. We've got to stop hyping these terrorist situations. . . . I think the message you have to get across is that the word 'exclusive' is a dirty word."[25]

The networks have cut back on scoop claims and some other forms of braggadocio, but the promotional habit should be suppressed completely in sensitive terrorism cases.

### Payola

In the unseemly competitive spirit that gripped television in the TWA case, the networks fell to accusing each other of using payola and checkbook journalism to get exclusive tapes and interviews. Once, the price of admission to the Amal's front lines was a cassette showing how the militiamen looked on television the previous night. But inflation touches everyone: by 1985, *Newsweek* reported one of its reporters was offered a tour of the TWA plane for $1,000, and several Amal tried to peddle a session with the hostages for $12,500. ABC denied paying for Glass's interviews with Berri and the hostages, and the *Washington Post's* Christopher Dickey concluded that ABC did not need to practice payola because of its longtime close contacts with the Amal.

Directly or indirectly, the networks bought tape from local Lebanese sources. Paying for pictures taken by free-lance photographers is standard practice for both newspapers and television; the validation of the material and the sources is usually known. But it becomes questionable when sources are murky and there is a suspicion that pictures have been produced and doctored by terrorists. In that case, the journalist is in the position of buying and then distributing tapes of doubtful authenticity and with a propaganda purpose. This should be rejected. Another danger in terrorist stories is that the lure of profits might stimulate gunmen to manipulate hostage situations and produce tapes especially for the television trade, another case in which standard journalistic practices need to be modified to fit nonstandard circumstances. Where a tape clearly confirms that a hostage is alive, and this is genuine news, then it can be used but only in an edited form accompanied by careful on-air explanations.

ABC's "Good Morning America" flew Mrs. Conwell to Cyprus, all expenses paid, for her chat with her husband and Berri. When the hostages finally were freed, NBC's "Today Show" paid plane and hotel costs to fly several families to West Germany for a reunion near the Frankfurt airport. Through what was described as a policy mix-up, CBS's "Morning News" also picked up a hotel tab for hostage family members it was interviewing. "Today's" producer, Steve Friedman, explained that getting the families together made "better television." It may have been better television, but it was terrible journalism in the context of a news story like the TWA hijacking. The reason is that it is rearranging reality to suit television's peculiar needs for drama, not to mention exclusivity. When ABC flew Mrs. Conwell to Cyprus and the families were flown to West Germany, television was not reporting; it was staging. It was interfering in a news event. This should not be repeated.

# 6 / Government and Public Opinion

At the height of the Vietnam War, when he would occasionally have a drink with a reporter in his seventh floor office, Secretary of State Dean Rusk would lower his reserve briefly and let his anger show. He was infuriated by the negative news reports pouring out of Saigon. He would explain that he was on the American side of the war, and then ask accusingly why reporters couldn't be on the same side. Lyndon Johnson frequently posed the same question less politely, while poking a reporter in the chest. Some fifteen years later, one could hear the echo at a conference on terrorism when Lord Chalfont, the journalist and former minister, asked: "Can we not simply accept the fact that we are at war with international terrorism, that there are two sides, ours and theirs? If their side prevails, our freedoms will disappear, and the first freedom to go will be freedom of the press. Is it too much to ask that, in a free society at war with international terrorism, the press should be on our side?"[1]

The question is disarmingly reasonable in appearance but actually bristles with subtle complexities and, like the Rusk-Johnson complaints, moves from mistaken assumptions to misleading conclusions. During the Bay of Pigs planning, for example, those of us who were covering the story did what the CIA's Richard Bissell told us to do and kept a tight lid on what was happening. President Kennedy said later he wished the press had not been so patriotic; public exposure might have steered him away from disaster. During the Vietnam War, it turned out that the "unpatriotic" reporting from Saigon was no more misleading than the "patriotic" reports on which Rusk was basing his criticism. It was official misjudgment, not morally indifferent journalism, which betrayed reality and policy. In judging the coverage of terrorism, therefore, it is important not to confuse patriotism with conformity to government strategy. Reporters and officials can have equally patriotic goals but develop conflicts because they have different civic duties and different perspectives.

Generally speaking, reporters should be citizens first and journalists second. This does not make them propagandists. It does not require them to favor the government—or oppose it. But neither does it condone putting their own interests ahead of everybody else's. What it does mean is that all of the natural urges that sweep over reporters in a big story—the zest for exclusives, the impulse to dramatize the effort, to heighten excitement, to beat the competition—must be subordinated to the larger needs of society. Peculiarly journalistic values cannot be palmed off as public values nor justified by the public's need to know. This is a fraud that only invites coercive reprisals. In terrorist incidents especially, good citizenship requires restrained, responsible reporting aimed not at entertainment or self-aggrandizement but only at providing essential, factual information. A number of issues are involved.

### Cooperating with Government

The media should cooperate with government efforts to resolve a terrorist crisis even though it means bending some hardened mind-sets. Thanks mainly to Vietnam and Watergate, journalism's traditional skepticism toward government was converted in the 1970s into a combative relationship. All young reporters were imbued with the idea they had to attack officials and challenge policies or lose their press cards. The feeling is less intense now, but it has not disappeared; the methods and sometimes even the motives of government are questioned automatically. And suspicions surge whenever secrecy is involved, in the CIA's counter-terror program, for example, where journalistic skepticism is compounded by a natural American aversion to covert action. Thus, in 1985, the *Washington Post* took considerable satisfaction in exposing a CIA-trained Lebanese team that, without approval, had killed more than eighty people in a failed attempt to assassinate the shadowy Sheikh Fadlallah. In Neil Livingstone's opinion, "Efforts by some in the media unnecessarily to denigrate police, FBI, and intelligence organizations in recent years, without proper regard to the critical frontline role they play in combating terrorism must be brought to an end."[2]

In hostage situations, newsmen should be willing to withhold information where it might be damaging. In the case of the *Washington Post*, Bradlee says, "We do consult with the government regularly about sensitive stories and we do withhold stories for national security reasons, far more often than the public might think."[3] During the TWA crisis, the networks withheld information in several instances, sometimes in response to personal calls from the secretary of defense or secretary of state. Reporters should also be willing to pass on information that might be helpful to the government's crisis managers, unless there are compelling reasons not to. The same principle should apply to tapes, including outtakes, that can sometimes assist authorities in tracking down terrorist suspects and in developing intelligence. There are strong reasons for non-cooperation in many news situations where a reporter's usefulness can be destroyed by even the appearance of collaboration. But where hostages are involved, this risk usually is less than the potential danger. The presumptive policy should be to cooperate.

### Non-Interference

A corollary of cooperation is non-interference. As Katherine Graham expressed it, the media need "to gather and reveal information without making things worse, without endangering the lives of hostages or jeopardizing national security." Grossman made the same point: "Television should not report information that will endanger either the victims of terrorism or those who are trying to put an end to a terrorist episode. In such instances reporters should without question seek the guidance of authorities."[4] No one can quarrel with these sentiments; the problem is that in real-life crises they are often lost in the crush of competition, deadline pressures, and coils of ambiguity about sources, facts, motives, and consequences.

In one instance, a Pentagon official leaks word about a Delta Force movement, and NBC is denounced because the leak was not authorized by the White House. In another case, leaks about a military buildup against Libya are encouraged because the White House wants to keep Gaddafi off balance. Leaks are sometimes used for political purposes, as in the early days of the Iranian hostage crisis, and sometimes denounced only because they are politically inconvenient. This process nourishes cynicism; it blurs issues that the CIA's William J. Casey tries to define in black and white terms; and it encourages the media to yield to their natural instinct to publish first and worry about consequences later.

But whatever the bureaucratic provocations may be, journalists should worry about consequences anyway, especially in terrorist incidents where lives are involved and the stakes are high. Despite all the manipulation of information and issues, reporters should check with the White House or whatever agency is in charge before publishing sensitive information. Grossman's advice on this point was right, even though he apparently did not follow it himself in making the Abbas interview decision. Contrary to myth, reporters will not lose their manhood if they explore the potential impact of a story before they break it. Also, the presumption should favor the government's view, first because it has the ultimate responsibility and, second, because the possibility of the press being misused by guileful officials is less important than protecting hostage lives.

In this connection, reporters need to show a great deal more restraint than their nature usually allows in reporting government strategy and plans. When they swarm over a story, they vacuum clean every news source they can locate in order to find out what is going on. This is the way they always operate, whether it is a city hall scandal or a summit conference. In terrorist crises, they inevitably dig out the government's strategy, its operational planning, and often even the secret intelligence methods being used, as in the case of the Berlin bombing. They then rush into print or onto the air with what they know. The result is that terrorists get a look at America's cards while they keep their own hidden. Admittedly, advance information sometimes is needed to inform a public debate. More often it is broadcast only because a reporter has it in hand, not because the public has any immediate need to know. In this case, journalists should put the national interest ahead of their own competitive desires.

## National Security

For a variety of reasons, including their historic relationship to wartime, the sensitivity of military secrets is more readily recognized by journalists than political planning. Yet these too are frequently spread out on television screens without much thought about consequences. The gathering momentum of decision-making leading up to the air attack on Libya could not be kept out of the news, even by the most conscientious reporters, because of the administration's extensive consultations with congressmen, allies, and others. Major policies also were involved so that informed discussions were necessary in advance of action.

But in specific terrorist cases it is difficult to see any justification for military disclosures. What public purpose was served by detailing the radio intercept and other intelligence methods used to connect Libya to the Berlin bombing? Why did television viewers—and terrorists—need to know immediately that the Delta Force and fleet were on the move in the TWA case? Even when some Pentagon official leaks information, it should be cross-checked with the State Department and White House to make sure the leak is intentional and will not interfere with official efforts to save hostages. Every Washington correspondent knows that the government is always getting its wires crossed and that what one official or agency is saying is not necessarily fact or policy. Crossed wires may be an excuse to run with a story; they are no justification for endangering lives or delicate negotiations.

## Government Action

It is suggested from time to time that the media would be encouraged in their good citizenship if the government imposed coverage restrictions in cases of terrorism. Journalists are immediately seized with convulsions, sickened by the threat to democracy, not to mention their desire for a carefree life, and we hear the familiar warning: "There must be no government restraints on freedom of the press." What is odd about this is that reporters are already swathed in government restrictions. On the White House beat, they are unable to move without a go-ahead from the presidential staff and the Secret Service. They also submit to the pooling of news and pictures. At the State Department, correspondents routinely accept the conditions officials specify when they disclose information—"off the record," "deep background," "background," "attributable to informed sources," or whatever. During the Geneva summit, several thousand newsmen watched the comings and goings on television and scrambled for trivia while Reagan and Gorbachev did their talking behind guarded doors. Television cameras were only recently allowed into the Congress, and still are barred from most courts. And authorities placed heavy restrictions on reporters trying to cover the *Challenger* disaster.

The point is that the media are constantly confronted with restrictions even in the routine coverage of news. And these are even more justified in terrorist events where gunmen are indifferent to the First Amendment and therefore hold an advantage over a democratic government that must respect it. When violent acts were the work of individuals or even small groups, which was the pattern in the 1960s and 1970s, they resembled other kinds of crime and tended to be treated as police stories. This was the case when members of a Muslim sect seized 135 hostages in Washington in 1977 and created a media circus that is still being debated. The situation is vastly changed now when the West is confronted with the new phenomenon of state terror. Terrorism is no longer a police story, if it ever was; it is a form of warfare, "strategic warfare on the cheap."[5] For some nations, it is an instrument of foreign policy and aggression. And this places the journalistic issues in a significantly different framework.

State terror operates in the twilight zone between peace and conventional wars and nuclear conflicts which the superpowers cannot wage. As Shultz says, it is "low intensity warfare" used as a "flanking maneuver" by adversaries who cannot prevail against America's military strength.[6] In a country of lawyers like the United States, everyone quibbles about definitions, whether a war is a "low intensity war," "limited war," "police action," or "counter-insurgency program." War correspondents accepted censorship as a matter of course during World War II, because it was a declared war. Their descendants resisted any curbs in Vietnam because it was not supposed to be a war. But definitions do not change the dying. Clausewitz would have no trouble identifying Libyan or Syrian attacks against U.S. citizens as a form of war.

Because state terrorism is warfare, journalists should be willing to accept some of the restrictions that have been traditional during wartime. For one thing, they should agree to a rule, which American and other correspondents have long accepted in Israel, that they will not broadcast or publish sensitive military information without prior government approval. This would include troop and fleet movements, military action plans, radio intercepts, surveillance results, and other information that might compromise intelligence sources.

Another preventive action would be for governments, in Western Europe for example, to bar live television coverage of terrorist incidents at airports and other sites under their control. This would have the effect of keeping terrorists off television without resorting to prior restraint of publication. Also, it would depart very little from present practice. Police barricades already are thrown up at disaster sites and even on presidential trips when there are major security problems.

Some critics favor even more drastic governmental steps to deprive terrorism of the "oxygen of publicity," as Prime Minister Thatcher put it. Even a defender of the First Amendment like David Broder is prepared to support legal action, if necessary, to deny terrorists any access to American television. In Ireland, terrorists already are kept off the "telly" under a law which allows the government to ban any broadcasts "likely to promote, or incite to, crime. . . ." The journalist Conor Cruise O'Brien, who originated the restriction when he was minister of posts and telegraphs, said, "We in the Irish state regard the appearance of terrorists on television as an incitement to murder."[7] In England, the British Broadcasting Company cancelled a documentary in 1985 when Margaret Thatcher appeared to object to an interview with the IRA's reputed chief of staff. This created a brief ruckus but, in fact, terrorists are rarely interviewed on British television, and English reporters are much more accepting of government limits than their American counterparts. John O'Sullivan of the London *Times* spoke for many of his colleagues when he said he was "perfectly prepared" to support a ban against television interviews with terrorists in Northern Ireland.[8]

The writer Edward J. Epstein would apply the same restrictions that Britain and other European countries impose in the coverage of criminal proceedings. The press would not be allowed, during an actual terrorist episode, to interview terrorists or hostages, and terrorist demands would be kept secret on security grounds, like ransom notes. In addition, he would ban any use of terrorist tapes until any police investigation is completed because they are like evidence in a crime. No truth would be lost to the public, Epstein notes, because hostage interviews, as an example, are given under duress and "may as likely further a false picture as the truth."[9]

Aside from the philosophical problem of extending the concept of prior restraint, legal curbs like this would be difficult to obtain from Europe's many legislatures and even more difficult to enforce. And they would have no chance of being adopted in the United States where the Constitution stands opposed to prior restraints on the press. Although the provocations are great in terrorism, censorship is a cure that sometimes hurts more than it helps.

One only has to reflect on the Vietnam experience. The freewheeling uncensored coverage of the war, the televised scenes of death and destruction, created enormous problems for military commanders in the field and for political leaders in Washington. But, exaggerated as some of the reporting was, and as damaging, the American people ultimately developed a surer instinct for a failed strategy than their elected leaders, and this compelled adoption of a more realistic policy. State terrorism is indeed warfare but, as Shultz says, it is "low-intensity." For all the dangers it poses to individual hostages or to society as a whole, it is still not a general war. Full wartime censorship, therefore, would be out of proportion to the problem.

What is needed are limited restrictions that do not involve prior government restraints on publication but do include: effective protection against the disclosure of sensitive plans and military information, media-government cooperation, and both direct and indirect measures to reduce terrorist access to television. To avoid more coercive action, which CIA Director William J. Casey and others have threatened, journalists themselves should take the lead in tightening their practices and eliminating abuses which only erode the public support on which their freedoms depend. In their own self-interest, they need to foster a spirit of cooperation with authorities who are trying to resolve crises—a spirit centered on media responsibilities rather than media rights, focused on the best interests of hostages and country rather than on news beats and exclusive interviews with fugitive terrorists.

## Of Canons, Codes, and Councils

If there were a census of people eager to improve the behavior of journalists, it would include everyone in government, the business community, the professions, and probably most of the general population. The public solicitude is so great that juries have been setting new all-time records in libel awards. Public officials who used to keep a wary distance are now suing the media at the drop of an unkind remark. Once-shy business executives are striking back when criticized. Senator Jesse A. Helms (R-N.C.) tried to buy CBS to "improve" its news coverage. Atlanta's Mayor Andrew Young, a former U.S. ambassador to the

United Nations, has suggested that First Amendment rights should perhaps be suppressed in times of crisis. And a variety of laws and regulations have been proposed on the theory that compulsion is the only way reporters can be motivated to better themselves.

Because of the First Amendment, however, the media's most knowledgeable critics have focused on two less drastic approaches: self-regulation and public criticism. The idea is that journalists would be a greater credit to society if they agreed on professional guidelines to govern their coverage of hostage crises and other sensitive news situations. And they would be more likely to adopt effective guidelines if they were constantly goaded by public criticism.

## Guidelines

The rush to write guidelines whenever social repairs are needed is a primitive instinct from which few Americans have ever escaped, an ancient Anglo-Saxon inheritance characterized by a nearly blind faith in the power of laws. It is the belief that all of life and death, from marital regulations to international affairs, or vice versa, can be legally defined, codified, and brought under rational control. It is a national trait that, except for the British, sets Americans apart from other societies. Tocqueville, an even better reporter than Dan Rather, was quick to notice this. In the United States, he observed, "the spirit of the law, born within schools and courts, spreads little by little beyond them; it infiltrates through society right down to the lowest ranks, till finally the whole people have contracted some of the ways and tastes of the magistrates."[10] After Tocqueville, with the rise of science and the cult of reason, Americans became even more dependent on laws for a secular system of ethics and justice. Then in the 1960s, a wave of egalitarianism, combined with self-centered individualism, carried this to new extremes, producing a revolution of rising entitlements and, with it, an incredible surge in litigation and other forms of what Thomas Erlich has called "legal pollution."

Newspapers were the chroniclers of protest but also the targets as the new public activism produced a flood of complaints from civil rights and special interest groups, lawsuits from the victims of reckless reporting, and rising public demands for fairer, more accurate, and better balanced coverage of the news. Editors, who pretend they are callously indifferent to criticism, were in reality sensitive to the attacks. A whole series of actions followed: adoption of free press–fair trial standards in many states, creation of joint press–bar committees, development of ethical codes for editorial staffs, and major campaigns against unfair or unethical practices sponsored by the American Society of Newspaper Editors (ASNE) and other professional organizations. "The press faces no greater problem than that created by public doubt about its adherence to high principles and ideals," said Claude Sitton in the foreword to *Playing It Straight,* an ASNE book on ethics. "Some accusations of unethical conduct are groundless. Others, unfortunately, are not. No thoughtful observer questions the need to achieve greater fidelity to accuracy, fairness and balance."

These problems, all related to a perceived crisis of credibility, are still far from solved, but as mentioned earlier, they have been a major preoccupation of newspaper editors for the last half dozen years. For a variety of reasons, there has been no comparable movement among newscasters. One explanation is that television does not have the same professional tradition or editorial orientation. The Radio Television News Directors Association is very different from the ASNE. Partly because of their regulatory heritage and related anti-trust fears, the networks also maintain an arm's-length relationship even on professional issues. They may cooperate with press–bar committees. They individually produce guidelines covering "ethics and standards," "conflicts of interest," and even "terrorism." Sample:

> There must be a delicate balance of our obligation to keep the public informed, our obligation to avoid being used, and our obligation not to exacerbate or sensationalize the situation. . . . Hampering negotiations between terrorists and the authorities will be avoided to lessen the possibility of making the situation worse. . . . Generally any direct communication from terrorists, or alleged terrorists, is to be reported to the authorities promptly.

While there is wide agreement on many standards, however, there is no strong collective commitment in the industry to give the standards professional context and psychological force. This is one reason why guidelines failed to prevent television's excesses during the TWA hijacking and NBC's Abbas interview. It is the reason why critics are missing the mark when they clamor for network agreement on new guidelines to assure more responsible behavior in a future hostage crisis. For the emphasis on guidelines is just as misplaced as the lawyers' excessive faith in laws. It was not the guidelines which newspaper editors adopted that changed editorial attitudes. It was a change in attitudes, forced by public pressure, that produced the guidelines. There was a general sense that much criticism of the press was valid and that it was in the press's own pragmatic self-interest to take corrective action. Without any summit meetings, votes, or legal contracts, a consensus emerged that generated peer group pressures that slowly jostled many editors toward higher journalistic standards. Guidelines were a result not a cause.

Another fact about guidelines that poses a problem is that they may be voluntary but they look and feel like laws; this makes them an irresistible lure for lawyers fishing for contingency fees. We worked hard to develop an ethical practice code at the *New York Daily News*. But we no sooner passed out copies to the staff than libel-chasing lawyers began analyzing and annotating them like a Supreme Court decision. They combed through every sentence looking for the slightest deviation between ideal and practice. Eventually, newspaper codes like ours were dragged into courtrooms, incorporated into decisions, and made into case law. Voluntary self-improvement efforts were converted into instruments of coercion. The law became a menace to guidelines that had been created, in many cases, in response to the law's complaints. Editors were nudged back toward Socrates's beloved oral tradition so there would be no written codes or even notes for lawyers to subpoena.

A related issue is professionalism. Intellectuals like Irving Kristol and Daniel J. Boorstin argue that journalists would be much more useful to the world if only they were professionals, shaped and certified by formal academic training and licensed, presumably, by some government authority. Kristol refers to journalism as an "underdeveloped profession" characterized by "amateurism" and a "naive and blithe non-intellectualism."[11] Other critics argue that the behavior of reporters would be improved immensely if they only had to submit to the same ethical discipline that governs doctors or lawyers. But even a quick peek into the secret files of medical and legal grievance committees reveals a sorry record. Journalistic ethics do not suffer by comparison with other professions. By itself, self-regulation is form without substance, a deceit wrapped in the legal tinsel Americans find so appealing. For conviction without rules is more effective than rules without conviction.

It is this conviction that is needed in television news—a systematic commitment to more responsible practices in the coverage of terrorism, news values that flow from social understanding and sensitivity, that automatically subordinate competition and dramatic effect to the national interest and distinguish between damaging disclosures and one-day scoops. The challenge, in other words, is not to write codes but to change the editorial value system on which codes ultimately depend for meaning and force. For this, the power of public opinion is necessary.

## Public Opinion

Public opinion has to be brought to bear on all the central issues raised in television's coverage of terrorism. This must be done in a sustained, focused, and forceful way so that the media—especially television, which now dominates the news scene—are under remorseless pressure to correct their faults. Canons and guidelines are the machinery of implementation; they can never be anything more than high-sounding words, like China's constitution, unless they are enforced by committed editors and producers and used not only in seminars but in the competitive heat of a major story. All the improvements we have been talking about in the coverage of terrorism—from a ban against broadcasting military secrets to the de-emphasis of hostages and families—can only happen if newscasters themselves are motivated to put them into effect. And the finest available motivator is the public itself.

Journalists, like all exemplars of professional arrogance, are notoriously slow learners. They did not change their coverage of blacks until riots and street demonstrations awakened them to the civil rights revolution. They never became sensitized to the new concerns and changing roles of women until the historic significance of the women's movement had already been recognized by nearly everyone else. But they learned eventually; public pressure generated by minorities, single-issue groups, politicians, businessmen, and many other complainants had an impact, changing news practices significantly. There will be more changes in the years to come, and again the principal instructor will be public opinion in all its guises, from single-issue protests and changing national attitudes to deeper social trends, but most easily identified perhaps in the form of criticism.

## Media Criticism

Although it is never welcome, criticism can be a powerful force for change and, under favorable circumstances, for improvement. This is particularly so when it reflects the public's own view, as it did in the TWA hijacking. In theory, criticism should flow freely through all the nooks and crannies of a democracy, but there are special problems in the case of the media. They are the bumptious critics of the world around them, but out of human weakness, they are slow to discover their own faults. And critics outside of journalism find it difficult to be heard because the media control the communications system through which complaints are relayed from one institution to another. It is, in short, a vicious circle: The media are necessary to transmit public criticism which, in turn, is needed to bring pressure on the media. Hence, the dilemma: how to get the media to submit to the same critical process they so enthusiastically inflict on others.

Sensitive to the problem, a number of editors have installed media critics in their newsrooms with instructions to be fearless. With a few notable exceptions—David Shaw of the *Los Angeles Times,* for example—their work has been neither fearless nor notable. The networks have media specialists but their output is so well hidden no one can think who they are. Another approach has been to create ombudsmen—in some cases outsiders imported from other walks of life—to keep watch on news practices at a newspaper, television station, or network. Two celebrated examples of this genre were Bill Green's brutal analysis of the Janet Cooke fake-story case at the *Washington Post* and Burton Benjamin's confession of CBS errors in the way General William Westmoreland was treated in a Vietnam documentary. Ombudsmen are not widely used, however, nor very successful. Newsmen just do not make very good ascetics.

A more promising approach to self-criticism is to cooperate with human nature. Instead of expecting individual newspapers, television stations, or networks to attack themselves, encourage them to attack their competitors. When journalism was younger, newspapers used to assault each other almost as often as they assailed politicians. Now there are fewer competitors and more inhibitions. A newspaper editor may be horrified by something a colleague has done but be reluctant to make a fuss about it. Network newscasters are less chummy, but they often react the same way out of a reasonable fear that any criticism of a rival will invite revenge. Charles Osgood of CBS was mildly critical of NBC's Abbas interview, but CBS itself and ABC resolutely refused to comment. Some of this shyness could be overcome if groups with grievances were more effective in applying the techniques of media manipulation to their cause. Although competition has been reduced to low levels in the newspaper business by local monopolies and group ownership, it still runs strong in television. With stimulation, it could be used to get professional performance messages sent from one television news team to another.

A splendid example was the payola issue that spilled all over the TWA story. "I have a problem," said Steve Friedman of the "Today Show," ". . . with ABC chartering a plane to fly Mrs. Conwell to Cyprus and then a week later saying it was wrong for us to fly families over for interviews. . . ."[12] Friedman would never have aired his "problem"—almost no one would have heard about it, certainly—if it had not been for the creative services of television critics on newspapers who nurtured the whole issue into a fine public controversy. Newspaper editors like to put their critics in the front lines in cases like this because they still dismiss television news as entertainment, but more important, because it allows them to publish criticism of a competitor without having to take any personal or institutional responsibility. When the networks complain, the editor simply shrugs helplessly. "Nothing I can do," he explains. "A critic can say what he wants to." This is a cop-out, of course, but the television critics do show that journalists, who are squeamish about criticizing members of their own club, are less reluctant to attack other clubs. Newspapers, therefore, can attack news practices in television; television can offer constructive suggestions to newspapers; and the news magazines, which never admit error, can keep watch on everybody.

In the payola cases, it happened that the newspapers were not handing out any free plane tickets, so they hurried into print to tell their readers all about the shocking things television was doing. In their customary search for controversy, reporters collected all the rumors they could find, rounded up charges and denials from assorted television executives, and soon had all three networks embroiled in a public quarrel. Critics like the *Washington Post*'s Tom Shales helped keep the spit turning with appropriate comments, and *Newsweek*, not worried about television or newspapers other than its *Washington Post* partner, took the story on a romp of its own. Payola began to look like an important public issue, and as expected, the networks took due and careful note. In the Abbas case, to cite another example, newspapers not only headlined the administration's denunciation of NBC but chimed in with their own criticisms and this time not only in their entertainment sections.

Audiences react directly to many of television's excesses—the exploitation of hostage families, for example—so that the networks do not always need newspapers to tell them they have stepped on a landmine. But newspapers still can be helpful. When they wade in with stories and critical comments, they can magnify public reactions and increase pressures on the networks to take corrective action. And in other circumstances, television can return the compliment, taking newspapers to task, for example, when they published intelligence methods used to link Libya to the discotheque bombing in Berlin. One branch of the media can be used to encourage another branch to climb toward ever higher plateaus of journalistic responsibility.

As they say in physics, however, this kind of self-generated inter-media criticism is a weak force; it must be bolstered and supplemented. Additional ways must be found to bring individual grievances, group protests, and public complaints to bear on journalism and to do this with enough force to prevail over professional habit and competitive priorities. The challenge can be looked at from at least three perspectives: government involvement, private watchdog groups, and public access to television.

## Government Involvement

Many of the great issues in journalism, certainly including news practices in the coverage of terrorism, are joined most conspicuously in the daily collisions between the media and government. There is a constant tension between the positive images officials want to create on the evening news shows and the foibles and follies that newscasters are forever reporting. The result is a running stream of official complaint and journalistic rebuttal.

Political leaders, from Congress to the White House, can give effective voice to their problems with the media. They have the platform and the public standing. Unlike many others in our society, they are able to command media attention and can often mobilize public support for their position. They were able, for example, to force changes in the Freedom of Information Act by arousing public concern over national security risks.

In recent years, particularly in the Reagan administration, government officials have been striking out somewhat more boldly than before against their media antagonists, even suing for libel or defamation of character in an attempt to redress wrongs and inflict punishment. General Westmoreland's libel suit against CBS would have been unthinkable even as recently as the 1960s. And no one could imagine an official of a foreign government, such as Israel's Ariel Sharon, going into a U.S. court against a media giant like *Time* magazine. The CIA's Casey did not have the slightest qualm about threatening to prosecute NBC and the *Washington Post* for stories about secret intelligence methods. No one doubted he reflected the president's personal view and would be supported by public opinion.

Journalists have decried this official assertiveness, charging as they always do that it has a "chilling effect" on the free flow of information. But why shouldn't officials, as well as private citizens, be able to strike back if they have been libeled or defamed? Why shouldn't the CIA try to force reporters to keep the lid on sensitive information? In short, why shouldn't the media be called to account for what they do, especially when they have become an integral part of the democratic process? No skies have fallen; there are no signs of any permanent damage to the republic. Lawsuits can be intimidating—especially for small newspapers and television stations—but our whole society is being ravaged by litigious excess; this is not just a journalistic threat. And at the national level, the power of the media has not been diminished; it has grown.

Indeed, it can be argued that the press has the advantage in the ceaseless struggles between press and government and that, if anything, Washington has been too timid rather than too harsh in its responses. The reasons are twofold. Political leaders are desperately dependent on television for everything they do, whether it is getting elected, communicating with constituents, or mobilizing support for their programs. Secondly, they fear television's power and therefore are extremely wary about questioning what it does. This could be seen even in the Casey attack. Although White House officials clearly felt just as strongly about press leaks as the CIA director, they shuddered at the thought of a legal confrontation with their media antagonists. So the threats of prosecution were melted down to pleas for cooperation.

Congressmen are even more cautious than members of the executive. Old-time political barons with safe seats and long seniority used to be able to sneer at reporters, but they are gone. Media access is now the lifeblood of politics; congressmen are pathetically dependent on snippets of television coverage just to prove they exist. Former Senator J. William Fulbright and Senator Daniel P. Moynihan have written trenchant critiques of the press. In his own zeal for media reform, of course, Senator Helms tried vainly to buy CBS. But these are exceptions to a general pattern of reticence. The law of political survival is to woo television, not to irritate it.

If Washington is to become a richer source of journalistic improvement, the impetus will have to come mainly from the public or, more specifically, from professional organizations, unions, trade associations, and special interest groups capable of mobilizing and focusing public attention on media-government issues. Most politicians need this kind of aid, as all lobbyists can testify, because they only like to exercise courageous leadership when they feel themselves being pulled along on a public tide. In the TWA hostage case, for example, the tide of complaint was running so strongly that a congressional committee felt it was politically safe to hold hearings on the way television had covered the story. And these produced some of the strongest criticisms to emerge in the controversy. The problem, of course, is how to convert this kind of episodic public appraisal into a continuing critical tradition aimed at improved media performance without government interference or coercion.

### Watchdog Groups

Special interest groups like the American Bar Association need to keep forcing their attention on media leaders so that important journalistic issues are kept on the public agenda and there is constant pressure for improvement. The Bar Association, for instance, led the drive some years ago to improve news practices in the coverage of trials. Press–bar committees were established all over the country, coverage guidelines were written, and significant changes in coverage patterns followed. The bar and professional news organizations also worked together to solve other mutual problems, many of them related to the First Amendment.

The Bar Association, incidentally, set off one of the sharper debates that developed over the TWA coverage. It was at its convention in London that Margaret Thatcher made her famous plea to the media for a "voluntary code of conduct" that would "starve the terrorist and hijacker of the oxygen of publicity on which they depend." At the same session, the State Department's legal adviser charged that the TWA coverage "gave irresponsibility and tastelessness a new meaning." And Attorney-General Edwin Meese talked cautiously about seeking ways to exploit the "mutual good will" already existing between the media and government. All of this produced a flurry of headlines and focused public attention on the issues.

Other special interest groups are working on problems such as television exit polling, which probably will be modified, and some of the think tanks that have proliferated in recent years have attacked a few media issues. The work of Stephen Hess at The Brookings Institution comes to mind. Some experts on terrorism, for example, Terrell E. Arnold, have not hesitated to deal harshly with the media's more egregious errors. But there is no central institutional focus of public complaint like the Press Council or Broadcasting Complaints Commission in Britain. With deregulation and other developments, the Federal Communications Commission has gone out of the program monitoring business. An independent National News Council, modeled after the British Press Council, died in 1984 after eleven years of fitful existence.

### News Councils

The National News Council was formed in 1973 in order "to make press freedom more secure by providing an independent forum for debate about media responsibility and performance, so that such debate need not take place in government hearing rooms or on the political campaign trail."[13] The need for public debate, aimed at self-correction rather than legislative coercion, was certified by the arrogant refusal of the media to open their own newspaper columns or broadcast time to their critics. During its troubled career, the council acted on more than two hundred complaints involving the television networks and national press as well as the small and weak. In the words of its last president, former CBS news chief Richard S. Salant, it produced "a body of sound case findings and a collection of useful studies of journalistic issues."[14] But when it finally died it was for lack of love. The council had been rejected by the great centers of media power. Its work was so ignored the public never knew how it was being served and could not even note the council's passing. Financial support disappeared and collapse followed.

In all of the postmortems by friend and foe, legal process was never mentioned; it should have been. At the time of the council's founding, much of the controversy over media accuracy and fairness centered on competing rights, and the legal profession was directly involved in the debate. Naturally, a legal model was regarded as the obvious choice for resolving issues in dispute. So the council was set up as a kind of tribunal and its first two chairmen were high-ranking jurists steeped in legal brine rather than journalism. In keeping with the adversary procedure so dear to the judiciary, the council sat in judgment while cases were called, evidence presented, witnesses testified, and plaintiffs and defendants argued. Just like a real court, except there was no law, no authority, no sanctions. Unlike a prosecutor, the council had neither the staff nor the power to probe deeply for facts that might challenge testimony. Defendant networks and newspapers submitted to the proceedings voluntarily, if at all. And the penalty of publicity could not be imposed on wrongdoers because the media—surprise—never found the council's actions very newsworthy.

The fact is that litigation is an uncertain route to truth or justice even under the best of circumstances; it is totally unsuited to resolving many of society's more subtle and difficult problems. If the council had begun its life in a less legalistic and threatening way—if it had dealt forcefully with issues instead of cases, as its Freedom of the Press Committee did in its later years, it might have been able to struggle toward professional acceptance; conceivably, in this way it could have extended its life long enough to become an effective force for journalistic improvement, and at a time when the profession itself was becoming less hostile to change.

The original need cited for the council is still valid: to give voice and public effect to grievances against the press so that they are channeled toward internal reform rather than toward government intervention. The idea should be revived. In a new incarnation, stripped of judicial pretense and centered on professional improvement, a council could yet fulfill its purpose. And the media should take the lead in making this happen. The current flood of libel suits and other forms of intimidation should be inspiration enough to support a forum for the public airing of journalistic problems. The industry is strong enough, certainly, to be less thin-skinned than it has been about criticism which it applies so enthusiastically to others. And it is rich; media-related foundations are groaning with money that could help finance a council. If the council idea were to be a reality again, there probably would be other assistance as well to broaden support and avoid any appearance of media domination.

There should also be greater support for other forms of media monitoring. Insider criticism in publications such as the *Washington Journalism Review* and *Columbia Journalism Review* does not reach enough people to generate any public pressure. Public interest organizations, for instance, should help sustain strongly independent organs of media analysis and criticism similar to the "Inside Story," which Hodding Carter produced on public broadcasting. Imaginative television programs like Fred Friendly's pioneering "Media and Society Seminars" should also be produced to illuminate media problems and help marshal public support for change.

### Public Access

Beyond government action and watchdog groups such as a national news council is another large issue: public access to television. The surge of libel actions and other attacks on the media is not just a symptom of unpopularity, which many reporters consider a badge of honor; it reflects a much more serious condition—the feeling of many leaders in many segments of society that they are being denied fair access to television, where the real business of democracy is now being transacted. Producers and news directors are pulling all the switches that decide who appears and who does not, who can plead his cause and who can reply to accusations. Citizens who believe they have a right to be heard, to present their views in their own way, cannot get to the microphones to speak. Television decision-makers are accused of exercising arbitrary power over the nation's affairs and then deciding how and by whom they themselves should be held accountable.

The issue is not as simple as critics state it; it would take a lot of modifiers to put it into full context. But there is a basic problem of accountability, and it calls for urgent action. Television simply has to provide more public access to what is, in many ways, a public resource. Its power is too great, its civic responsibilities too large, to hold all that it does in a private preserve. Talk shows give the illusion of a free and varied flow of opinion, but in most cases, they are produced by the networks or local stations themselves and the views of guests are shaped by the questions of interviewers. Commentators are paraded on and off screen, not on their own initiative, but only because they are needed to explain a big story. A Soviet propagandist appears on national television to rebut a presidential speech because he is invited; an American expert with more impressive credentials is never seen nor heard, because he is not invited. And beyond the news shows is the great Sargasso sea of television drama where faceless writers and producers present their own cultural, moral, and even political views with only Nielsen ratings for a guide. It was a rare episode of "MASH" that did not make a political or social point. The "Quincy" series specialized in delivering dramatized editorials on topical public issues. Television calls all the shots on what is seen and heard.

It is high time that the networks use their creative talents to open their airways to critics and others whose voices should be heard without translation into televese. Any number of approaches come to mind—video op-ed pages, letters to the anchor, guest editorials, filmed rebuttals, and truly independent critics who are free to bite their hosts, if necessary. There have been some panel discussions about television's performance in hostage cases, for example, but they were neither very critical nor penetrating; a skilled, free-swinging analyst could have been much more effective. Some devices such as guest editorials are being tried, on a local level at least, and a few shows like Don Hewitt's "60 Minutes" dare to read critical letters. In 1986, CBS ran a movie called "News at Eleven," which provided a brutally candid insight into the conflict between serious journalism and show business hype. But the total public access effort is far too limited and too grudging to satisfy the need.

The problems for television are, of course, major. For many reasons, it is essential that the networks maintain editorial control over presentation of the news. There are severe time constraints and difficult choices to make about who should get what time is available. Neglecting the access issue, however, could confront television with even larger problems—a growing disposition among the dispossessed to sue and, among the networks' many enemies, an incessant demand for government action to curb real or imagined abuses. Public broadcasting came into existence because of a perceived need for alternatives to commercial broadcasting. It is not terribly difficult to imagine pressures for a government network, an outgrowth of C-Span perhaps, to meet unmet needs for public access. In this atmosphere, it is in commercial television's interest to act first.

### Toward a Better Way

Whether it is increased public access or multiplying lawsuits, more vigorous media criticism or greater activism by public interest groups, the common goal is to mobilize the forces of public opinion to compel journalism to search for a better way. What needs to be done to weaken television's alliance with terrorism can only be done with the public's help. For the problems lie deep in the nature of television and in the culture of news, in instincts, habits, and competitive impulses that create unbearable tensions between ideals and practice, between press privileges and press responsibilities—tensions that cannot be reduced by the media alone. Journalists and the public are always being separated, like boys and girls at a high school dance, defined by their differences and their antagonisms rather than their identities. Yet the paradox is that they are both separate and at the same time one. The newscasters and producers who work for television are also members of the public. They sense the conflict between what they feel about terrorists and how they cover terrorists, yet they are held hostage by their own process, television's insatiable need for entertainment, illusion, drama, celebrities, immediacy, and pace.

If a man is to bring this invention under rational control, if news practices are to be brought into line with news responsibilities, then the general public and those members of the public who are journalists must be joined together in the effort.

# 7 / Preventive Journalism

In some ways, the debate about television's alliance with terrorism is out of focus. It is centered for the most part on emotional and operational issues. It is silent on the more fundamental failings of American journalism, a journalism that is more interested in violence than in the causes of violence. The irony is that these failings, more than hostage interviews or terrorist pictures, have contributed in indirect but detectable ways to some of the very crises that have attracted so much critical attention.

The long Iranian hostage ordeal might never have happened, for example, if the media had been scouting ahead for signals of unrest instead of nibbling canapes with the shah near the Peacock Throne. Americans were held hostage not by radical students but by a colossal ignorance of Iranian society and history that the press had done nothing to correct. In a devastating critique, Columbia University's Edward W. Said observed that reporters covering the Middle East usually are incredibly uninformed about Muslim culture, seldom know the languages, file reports in terms of American interests rather than a country's own internal life, and always seek out action in preference to significant observation.

The car-bombing of the marine barracks in Beirut is another case in point. Would the marines have been attacked, or would they even have been stationed where they were, if the media had alerted the American people in advance to the dangers hidden in hasty policy decisions? The marines were sent as a supposedly neutral peacekeeping force. But they were sent in the context of the Israeli invasion and were later committed on the side of the Christian Phalangists in their struggle against the Muslims. As Peter Jennings pointed out during a post-mortem exchange with David Broder, the United States suddenly "chose sides in a civil war." Under the circumstances, he suggested, the bombing could be described as an act of war rather than a terrorist attack.[1] Even more important, it might never have occurred if Washington had been deterred from its decision by timely warnings from those anchormen who sound so omniscient on the evening news.

As in all other things, Americans assume their journalism is superior to any other in the world and that they are adequately informed. But we have been surprised too often by the twists and turns of world events—caught too many times in the ambushes of history—to be so arrogantly complacent. The fact is that many of the most fateful issues facing the nation lie beyond the reach of our television and newspapers because our reporting system specializes in action and confrontation instead of the more subtle determinants of history. Whereas it is superbly equipped to cover a disaster after it has occurred—the wreckage and turmoil that followed the marine bombing—it is poorly prepared to identify the precursors of disaster in time for society to take preventive action if it can.

Yet this has to be one of the critical tests of a journalistic tradition—its ability to probe for the undercurrents of change in its own society and in the world generally so that the public can form timely and accurate judgments for its own protection. It is a test the media regularly fail. Indeed, they have missed some of the most momentous developments of the postwar period, in the United States as well as elsewhere, because their mind-set emphasizes instant action over social change, immediate visual events over primordial forces that cannot be photographed. In one of the most revealing comments made during the terror coverage debate, a network correspondent noted that it was only in times of disaster that television reporters get enough airtime to provide "context and perspective." In other words, the bombings have to happen before we can be told why they are likely to occur.

What is needed more than new rules for covering terrorism, therefore, is a new journalism. A preventive journalism that is always searching ahead of today's breaking news for the secret pockets of misunderstanding, the undetected human tensions that will burst onto the evening news shows next week or a year later. "There is little analysis of the bewildering harvest of facts each day brings in and there is far less evaluation," says Harvard's Stanley Hoffmann. "The intellectual and civic roles the press ought to play thus go begging. . . ."[2] Given their power and public responsibility, reporters must be more than the sentinels of reaction, waiting to cover violence and disaster while another unseen world throbs with warnings we do not hear. They need to lead us into that world and help us detect the sounds of future crises even when our attention is naturally locked onto the immediate, the obvious, and the concrete.

This would require a sea change in philosophy. Definitions of news would have to be revised to emphasize thought as well as action, harmony as well as conflict, explanation as well as exposure. Television's visual and theatrical techniques, which mesh so well with violence, would have to be adapted to less photogenic subjects. In the case of foreign affairs, correspondents would need language skills, specialized training, and long-term commitments to a country or region. They would have to look deeply into societal trends on a sustained basis, even though this might mean less frequent spot appearances on showcase news shows. All of this would involve a large investment of money, time, and corporate interest. It would also mean coping with the natural resistance of readers and viewers who are more attuned to immediate visual action than invisible future threats.

Yet, just as scientists press out into new frontiers of knowledge, so should journalists venture beyond old conventions to develop new and better ways to inform society. The tradition of reactive reporting needs to give way to an anticipatory philosophy that seeks to prevent disasters, not merely report them. In the long run, this will do more than new ethical codes to promote restraint and responsibility in the coverage of terrorism.

To consider all that is wrong with journalism today is to despair. To reflect on the progress that has been made in the years since blacks were called "cheap addresses" is to have hope.

# Notes

**Chapter 1**

1. Excerpts reproduced in Uri Ra'anan, Robert L. Pfaltzgraff, Jr., Richard A. Shultz, Ernst Halperin, and Egor Lukes, *Hydra of Carnage* (Lexington, Mass.: Lexington Books, 1986), pp. 488-91.

2. From a memoir by Karim Pakradouni, quoted by Fouad Ajami in "Lebanon and its Inheritors," *Foreign Affairs*, Spring 1985, p. 785.

3. Henry Kissinger, "The Impact on Negotiations—What the Experts Say," *TV Guide*, September 21, 1985; ABC "Nightline," July 25, 1985.

4. Center for Communication seminar, October 23, 1985; interview with David Broder.

5. Quoted by Tom Shales, "Television's Excesses, On Screen and Off," *Washington Post*, July 1, 1985.

6. Interview with Fred Friendly.

7. Center for Communication seminar.

**Chapter 2**

1. "Mondale Farewell," *The New York Times*, November 8, 1984; "The Medium and Mondale," *The New York Times*, November 9, 1984.

2. "Two Guards of Marcos, Back from Hawaii, Tell of the Final Hours," *The New York Times*, March 11, 1986.

3. Charles Krauthammer, "Looking Evil Dead in the Eye," *Time*, July 15, 1985.

4. Interview with Elaine Sciolino.

5. David A. Stockman, *The Triumph of Politics* (New York: Harper & Row, 1986), p. 7.

6. "Moscow's Vigorous Leader," *Time*, September 9, 1985.

7. "The Intrusion of Television in the Hostage Crisis," *The New York Times*, June 26, 1985, *Washington Post*, July 1, 1985.

8. "How TV's Power Has Again Transformed Public Opinion," *Washington Post*, October 22, 1984.

9. Lloyd Cutler, "Foreign Policy on Deadline," *Foreign Policy*, Fall 1984.

10. Tufts University symposium, February 28-March 1, 1986.

11. Radio-Television News Directors Association Convention, quoted in "News Directors on the Defensive in Nashville," *Broadcasting*, September 16, 1985.

## Chapter 3

1. Alexis de Tocqueville, *Democracy in America*, Vol. II (New Rochelle, N.Y.: Arlington House), p. 122.

2. See Daniel Bell's essay on "Technology, Nature, and Society," in *The Winding Passage* (Cambridge, Mass.: Abt Books, 1980), pp. 34 ff.

3. Interview with Richard C. Wald.

4. "The Beirut Hostages—ABC and CBS Seize an Opportunity," *Public Opinion*, August/September 1985, pp. 45 ff.

5. "The Coverage Itself—Why it Turned into Terrorvision," *TV Guide*, September 21, 1985; interview with Edwin Diamond.

6. Interview with John Chancellor.

7. "Networks Turn Eye on Themselves," *Washington Post*, June 30, 1985.

8. Churchill Lecture, London, December 6, 1985.

9. Alexander Haig, Jr., "TV Can Derail Diplomacy," *TV Guide*, March 9, 1985.

10. Confidential source.

11. Interview with Robert B. Oakley.

12. UPI, June 23, 1985.

13. Benjamin C. Bradlee, "The Press is not Reckless About National Security," *Washington Post*, National Weekly Edition, June 23, 1986.

14. Katherine Graham, Churchill Lecture, London, December 6, 1985.

15. Neil C. Livingstone, *The War Against Terrorism* (Lexington, Mass.: Lexington Books, 1982), p. 68.

16. Theodore H. White, *America in Search of Itself* (New York: Harper & Row, 1982), p. 182.

17. Krauthammer, "Looking Evil Dead in the Eye."

18. National Advisory Committee on Criminal Justice Stan-

dards and Goals, Task Force on Disorders and Terrorism, Washington, 1976, p. 9 of report.

19. Livingstone, *The War Against Terrorism*, p. 59.

20. "Networks Turn Eye on Themselves," *Washington Post*, June 30, 1985.

21. "The Intrusion of Television in the Hostage Crisis," *The New York Times*, June 26, 1985.

22. "Shiite Spin Control," *New Republic*, July 15-22, 1985, p. 10.

## Chapter 4

1. Jerusalem Conference on International Terrorism, July 2-5, 1979, excerpts published in *Political Communication and Persuasion*, Vol. 1, No. 1, 1980, p. 95.

2. Ibid., p. 80.

3. Daniel J. Boorstin, *The Image* (New York: Atheneum, 1977), p. 12.

4. Richard Clutterbuck, *Living with Terrorism* (London: Faber and Faber, 1975), p. 147.

5. Tom Shales, "TV's Great Hostage Fest," *Washington Post*, June 29, 1986.

6. Lawrence K. Grossman address, "Television and Terrorism: A Common Sense Approach," at the Davos Symposium, February 1, 1986.

7. Ibid.

8. Interview with Hodding Carter.

9. Interview with David Gergen.

10. Ibid.

11. Livingstone, *The War Against Terrorism*, p. 58.

12. Ibid., p. 65.

13. Interview with Richard Wald.

14. Interview with John Chancellor.

15. Grossman, "Television and Terrorism: A Common Sense Approach."

16 "America's Ordeal by Television," *Washington Post*, July 2, 1985.

17. David Pearl, Lorraine Bouthilet, and Joyce Lazar, eds., *Television Behavior: Ten Years of Scientific Progress and Implications for the Eighties* (Washington, D.C.: U.S. Government Printing Office, 1982).

18. "As Violence Thrives, the Debate Goes On," *The New York Times*, April 6, 1986.

19. Alexis de Tocqueville, *Democracy in America,* Anchor edition (New York: Doubleday & Co., 1969), Vol. I, p. 9.

20. Cutler, "Foreign Policy on Deadline," p. 114.

21. Interview with Richard Wade.

22. Jody Powell, *The Other Side of the Story* (New York: William Morrow and Company, 1984), p. 238.

23. Cutler, "Foreign Policy on Deadline," p. 117.

24. Interview with Robert B. Oakley.

25. Interview with Richard C. Holbrooke.

26. Symposium, Electronic Media, July 11, 1985.

27. Neil C. Livingstone and Terrell E. Arnold, eds., *Fighting Back* (Lexington, Mass.: Lexington Books, 1986), p. 249.

28. Ronald Steel, *Walter Lippman and the American Century* (Boston: Little, Brown and Company, 1980), p. 449.

## Chapter 5

1. Jody Powell, "Rating the Press," Los Angeles Times Syndicate, June 30, 1985.

2. Krauthammer, "Looking Evil Dead in the Eye."

3. Cutler, "Foreign Policy on Deadline," p. 127.

4. Interview with Richard Wald.

5. Margaret Thatcher speech, *Washington Post,* July 16, 1985.

6. ABC's "Nightline," June 25, 1985.

7. Interview with John Chancellor.

8. J. Bowyer Bell, *A Time of Terror* (New York: Basic Books, 1978), p. 116.

9. Interview with John Chancellor.

10 David Broder, Center for Communication seminar.

11. Lawrence K. Grossman, memorandum, July 24, 1985.

12. Henry Kissinger, "The Impact on Negotiations—What the Experts Say."

13. Peter Jennings, Center for Communication seminar.

14. W. D. Livingstone, in Livingstone and Arnold, eds., *Fighting Back,* p. 214.

15. Ibid., p. 217.

16. Grossman, "Television and Terrorism: A Common Sense Approach."

17. Fred Friendly address, Center for Strategic & International Studies, Georgetown University, October 9, 1985.

18. Grossman, "Television and Terrorism: A Common Sense Approach."

19. Kissinger, "The Impact on Negotiations—What the Experts Say."

20. "TV Examines its Excesses," *Time*, July 22, 1985.

21. Charles Glass, "The Crisis Coup," *Washington Journalism Review*, September 1985.

22. Interview with John Chancellor.

23. Grossman, "Television and Terrorism: A Common Sense Approach."

24. Ibid.

25. Testimony by Fred Friendly before the House Foreign Affairs Committee, July 30, 1985.

### Chapter 6

1. Benjamin Netanyahu, ed., *Terrorism, How the West Can Win* (New York: Farrar, Strauss, Giroux, 1986), p. 235.

2. Livingstone, *The War Against Terrorism*, p. 75.

3. Bradlee, "The Press is not Reckless About National Security."

4. Graham, Churchill Lecture; Grossman memorandum.

5. Livingstone and Arnold, eds., *Fighting Back*, p. 3.

6. Address, National Defense University, January 15, 1986.

7. Broadcasting Authority, Amendment No. 37 (16), p. 1863; Conor Cruise O'Brien, quoted in Benjamin Netanyahu, ed., *Terrorism, How the West Can Win*, p. 232.

8. Ibid.

9. "Terrorism: What Should We Do?" *This World*, No. 12, Fall 1985, p. 44.

10. de Tocqueville, *Democracy in America*, Anchor edition, p. 270.

11. "The Underdeveloped Profession," *The Public Interest*, Winter 1967, p. 44.

12. Tom Shales, "America's Ordeal by Television," *Washington Post*, July 2, 1985.

13. National News Council, *In the Public Interest: III* (New York: The National News Council, 1984), p. xiii.

14. Ibid., p. xvii.

### Chapter 7

1. Center for Communication seminar.

2. Stanley Hoffmann, *Primacy or World Order* (New York: McGraw-Hill Book Company, 1978), p. 232.